ROMANTICISM AND TRANSCENDENTALISM

(1800–1860)

Jerry Phillips, Ph.D.
General Editor

Department of English
University of Connecticut, Storrs

Michael Anesko, Ph.D.
Adviser and Contributor

Director, Honors Program in English
Pennsylvania State University

Jerry Phillips, Ph.D.
Andrew Ladd, Ph.D.
Principal Authors

Facts On File
An imprint of Infobase Publishing

Romanticism and Transcendentalism (1800–1860)

Facts On File, Inc.
An imprint of Infobase Publishing
132 West 31st Street
New York NY 10001

Library of Congress Cataloging-in-Publication Data

Phillips, Jerry (Jerry R.)
  Romanticism and transcendentalism : 1800–1860 / Jerry Phillips.
      p.   cm.—(Backgrounds to American literature)
  Includes bibliographical references and index.

  ISBN 0–8160–5668–4 (alk. paper)

  1. American literature—19th century—History and criticism.
  2. Romanticism—United States. 3. Transcendentalism (New England)
  I. Title. II. Series.

  PS217.R6P57 2005
  810.9'145—dc22   2005021490

Acknowledgments
pp. 11, 21, 27, 39, 51, 63, 67, 75, 81: Library of Congress, Prints and Photographs Division
p. 47: Fruitlands Museums, Harvard, MA

DEVELOPED AND PRODUCED BY DWJ BOOKS LLC

CONTENTS

PREFACE

The five volumes of *Backgrounds to American Literature* explore 500 years of American literature by looking at the times during which the literature developed. Through a period's historical antecedents and characteristics—political, cultural, religious, economic, and social—each chapter covers a specific period, theme, or genre.

In addition to these six chapters, readers will find a useful timeline of drama and theatrical history, poetry and prose, and history; a glossary of terms (also identified by SMALL CAPITAL LETTERS throughout the text); a biographical glossary; suggestions for further reading; and an index. By helping readers explore literature in the context of human history, the editors hope to encourage readers to further explore the literary world.

1. THE INTELLECTUAL AND SOCIAL FOUNDATIONS OF ROMANTIC THOUGHT

From the late eighteenth century to the end of the nineteenth century, in both Europe and the United States, an artistic and intellectual movement called ROMANTICISM became a dominant force in politics, religion, and the arts. Although the term *romanticism* means different things to the poet, minister, philosopher, political theorist, or artist, some basic principles apply to them all.

Principles of Romanticism

Romanticism was a reaction against convention. As a political movement, this reaction was reflected in the new democratic ideals that opposed monarchy and feudalism. In art, it meant a turn away from NEOCLASSICISM and the ancient models of Greek perfection and CLASSICAL correctness. Philosophically, romanticism would contend with RATIONALISM—the belief that truth could be discerned by logic and reason.

Romanticism asserted the power of the individual. Romanticism marked an era characterized by an idealization of the individual. Politically, the movement influenced democratic ideals and the revolutionary principles of social equality. Philosophically, it meant that the idea of objective reality would give way to subjective experience; thus, all truth became a matter of human perception. In the art world, romanticism marked a fascination with the individual genius, and elevated the artist, philosopher, and poet above all others.

Romanticism reflected a deep appreciation of the beauties of nature. For the romantics, nature was how the spirit was revealed to humankind. The romantic philosophers believed in the METAPHYSICAL or spiritual nature of reality. They thought that a higher reality existed behind the appearance of things in the physical world. Nature appeared to people as a material reality; however, because it evoked such strong feelings in humankind, it revealed itself as containing a higher, spiritual truth. Romantic artists tried to capture in their art the same feelings nature inspired in them.

Romanticism emphasized the importance of the subjective experience. The romantics believed that emotion and the senses could lead to higher truths than either reason or the intellect could. Romantics supposed that feelings, such as awe, fear, delight, joy, and wonder, were keys that could unlock the mysteries of the world. The result was a literature that continually explored the inward experiences of the self. The imagination became one of the highest faculties of human perception, for it was through the imagination that individuals could experience transcendent or spiritual truths.

Finally, romanticism was idealistic. On one hand, romanticism was philosophically rooted in idealism. Reality existed primarily in the ideal world—that is, in the mind—while the material world merely reflected that universe. In other words, the ideal world was "more real" than the real world. On the other hand, romanticism was literally idealistic; it tended to be optimistic in its outlook on life. Political and social romantics asserted that human beings could live according to higher principles, such as the beliefs in social equality, freedom, and human rights.

When studying the influence of these principles of romantic thought in the United States from 1800–1860, it is important to look also at some of the historical, philosophical, and artistic movements in Europe. European thought constantly made its way into American thought, and vice versa. In fact, there seemed to be an ongoing dialogue between the Old World and New over the character and nature of romanticism. The New World was intent on applying romantic principles to the uniqueness of the American experience. For its part, the Old World saw romanticism as a continuation of its long history and deep traditions.

❧ THE QUOTABLE GOETHE ❧

One of the most influential figures on both European and American romanticism was Johann Wolfgang von Goethe (1749–1832). A renaissance man, Goethe was a respected scientist and an accomplished writer. He wrote plays, poetry, and novels, deeply affecting the direction of each genre in literary history. Goethe's incredibly productive literary career has also made him one the most quotable figures in German history.

Indeed, many of Goethe's romantic ideas made their way into the romantic's lexicon by way of his uncanny knack for crafting a well-turned phrase, whose meanings come across even in translation. His aphorisms are quoted often and give perfect expression to certain romantic ideals:

> *So divinely is the world organized that every one of us, in our place and time, is in balance with everything else.*

> *One ought, every day at least, to hear a little song, read a good poem, see a fine picture, and if it were possible, to speak a few reasonable words.*

> *All truly wise thoughts have been thought already thousands of times; but to make them truly ours, we must think them over again honestly, till they take root in our personal experience.*

> *The best government is that which teaches us to govern ourselves.*

> *Beauty is a manifestation of secret natural laws, which otherwise would have been hidden from us forever.*

> *Thinking is easy, acting is difficult, and to put one's thoughts into action is the most difficult thing in the world.*

> *If you treat an individual as if he were what he ought to be and could be, he will become what he ought to be and could be.*

————————

Social and Political Romanticism

The French Revolution of 1789 created a torrent of romantic ideals across Europe. Unlike the American Revolution and the struggle for independence from an outside, imperial power, the French Revolution marked an internal struggle within one of Europe's great nations. The conflict was over social class and competing political ideologies, ideas that were indeed threatening and revolutionary. Because of the French Revolution, all of the principles of romanticism suddenly became a basis of government. The cry of the French revolutionaries for fraternity, equality, and liberty shook the foundations of the European monarchies. Common people had come to believe in the RIGHTS OF MAN. The European world tried to understand the causes of the French Revolution and what its greater implications were for humankind.

The French Revolution inspired many romantic writers to think of history as an evolution to a higher state. The French Revolution seemed to herald a rebirth of human possibility. In the old way of thinking, history was a static pyramid. It was a hierarchy, a GREAT CHAIN OF BEING, that flowed from God, down to kings, to common people, and then to the natural world. In the new way of thinking, history was freer flowing. It was viewed as a purposeful, moral voyage. It told the story not of kings and heroes, but of democracies, the will of the people, and the triumph of the individual.

Thomas Carlyle and Social Romanticism

One of the great thinkers of social romanticism was Thomas Carlyle (1795–1881). In his best-selling book *The History of the French Revolution* (1837), Carlyle provides the definitive romantic view of the Revolution. In highly romantic language, Carlyle dramatizes the plight of the French aristocracy but shows that ultimately they are victims of history. Carlyle makes real the characters of Louis and Marie Antoinette, giving the reader a strong identification with their plights. Nevertheless, he pits these "characters" against the tide of history. History, for Carlyle, is a living thing; indeed, he constantly refers to it as if it is one of the characters in the drama. Even History is surprised by the outcome of the revolution:

> But what if History were to admit, for once, that all the
> Names and Theorems yet known to her fall short? That this

❧ THE LIFE OF MARIE ANTOINETTE ❧

Marie Antoinette (1755–1793) was married to Louis XVI at the age of 14 (he was 15) in an arranged marriage between Austrian and French royalty. Being foreign born did not endear her to the "third estate"—the so-called middle class and peasantry in France that existed below the clergy (first estate) and nobility (second). She was, by most accounts, a scapegoat for the country's severe financial problems, which were at least in part, ironically, the result of financial support of the American Revolution by French royalty.

Throughout her reign, she was the victim of unkind and unflattering portrayals among the people. For example, when told that the peasants had no bread, she supposedly replied "let them eat cake," but there is no evidence that she ever expressed such a sentiment. She bore the brunt of the anti-aristocratic popular sentiment of the day. Stories of her unfaithfulness to Louis XVI were rampant—largely because the populace wanted to believe Louis was a cuckold and fool. Pamphlets were circulated citing all sorts of immoral behavior on her part. On July 14, 1789, a huge crowd of Parisians rushed to the Bastille, a state prison that had become a symbol of the despotism of the aristocracy. On October 6, a mob (that included women) stormed the palace and looted the queen's apartment. Hatred for the queen reached a fevered pitch, leading Thomas Jefferson, the American envoy to France at the time, to declare: "had there been no Queen there would have been no Revolution." In August 1792, the royal family was imprisoned. Both Marie and Louis were tried and executed: Louis in January, 1793, Marie in October of that year. Marie was bound, placed in a cart, and paraded through crowds on the way to the guillotine, her humiliation complete.

---

grand Product of Nature was even grand, and new, in that it came not to range itself under old recorded Laws-of-Nature at all; but to disclose new ones?

The French Revolution was singularly important because, in this new page in history, humankind is presented with a radically different notion of itself.

It is a change such as History must beg her readers to imagine, undescribed. An instantaneous change of the whole

body-politic, the soul-politic being all changed; such a change
as few bodies, politic or other, can experience in this world.

For Carlyle, history tells the story of the divine soul acting on human
affairs. In this chapter of human history, the spirit of romanticism de-
scended on the earth in the form of revolution. Carlyle thought that
humankind had been divinely ordained to think of itself in terms of
its higher spiritual nature, under the new principles of fraternity,
equality, and liberty.

Carlyle's works become highly influential in America, especially in
the thought of the Transcendentalists in general and Ralph Waldo
Emerson in particular. For these Americans, American History seemed
to be unfolding exactly in the way that Carlyle describes the French
Revolution. America, too, appeared to be acting out its own drama of
divine history.

Philosophical Romanticism

One cannot understand the complexities of American romanticism
and TRANSCENDENTALISM without at least a general understanding of
eighteenth-century philosophers Jean Jacques Rousseau
(1712–1778) and Immanuel Kant (1724–1804).

The French philosopher Jean Jacques Rousseau argued that civilization was creating a human race that was out of step with nature.
Civilization stripped people of their natural instincts. "Everything is
good when it leaves the hands of the Creator," he wrote, "everything
degenerates in the hands of man." Rousseau believed human beings
had innate intuitive powers; that is, they instinctively knew how to deal
with the outside world. He felt that so-called "primitive" people, those
who lived closer to and in harmony with nature, had a greater, more
refined intuition than "civil" human beings. Rousseau believed that
there were basic principles, such as liberty and equality, which were
innate to human beings. Civilization and governments, however, had
conditioned man to endure life without them. Rousseau's ideas were
influential to many, from the American and French revolutionaries to
romantic writers. His ideas of nature and intuition were taken even further in the philosophy of Kant.

Philosophy before Kant was largely based on rationalism and empiricism. RATIONALISM was the belief that knowledge of the world could
be obtained only through reason. Reason could know reality indepen-
dently from sense experience; that is, logic, not emotion, led to truth.
EMPIRICISM was its exact opposite. English philosophers, such as
John Locke (1632–1704) and David Hume (1711–1776), argued

that sense experience was the only way of arriving at knowledge. To get at the truth, one had to go by experience—by scientifically weighing the evidence.

Kant argued against both. He believed that the human mind was more than simply the sum of worldly experiences; rather, the mind contains innate structures or "categories" that enable it to actively organize the outside world in a comprehensible way. We know these categories by the human faculty known as INTUITION. Kant suggested that human beings could instinctively know the truth of something without conscious reasoning or rational thought. Kant called his philosophy "Transcendental philosophy," because one "transcends," or goes beyond, rationality or sense perception. Using intuition, one can see beyond physical Nature and into what he saw as a higher truth, the spiritual world.

Romantic writers, in the early nineteenth century, agreed with Rousseau, claiming that those intense experiences of natural scenes and dramas (such as mountains and storms) would reawaken the intuitive powers, particularly imagination. They agreed, too, with Kant's proposition that individuals contained within themselves an inborn spiritual knowledge. Romanticism celebrated the divinity of the individual. It assumed that individuals might have an *immediate* relationship to God, insofar as they placed themselves within Nature. The romantics believed that human nature was made in "likeness to God." They felt that communion with Nature would reveal the divinity of human beings as a higher, intuitive truth.

❧ SIR ISAAC NEWTON ❧

Romanticism departed from the dominant school of natural philosophy in the eighteenth century, which was largely derived from the natural science of Sir Isaac Newton (1642–1727). In his famous Principia *(1687), Newton had argued that the "phenomena of nature" could be rationally understood in terms of "the science of mechanics." In essence, he suggested, Nature was a great machine that operated on mathematical or necessary laws. The machine of Nature was viewed as self-sustaining. God was the First Cause or Prime Mover of the machine, but was not contained in it. God was the clockmaker who had designed a self-winding clock. While the alternative view held that God could and would change the "laws of nature" through miracles, Newton's physics suggested otherwise. The universe worked according to unchanging, irrefutable laws.*

Newton's ideas influenced thought for centuries. In philosophy, they led to an emphasis on mechanism, empiricism, and rationalism—all of these "isms" supported a scientific understanding of the nature of reality. His ideas were applied to economics and theology, and even politics. This influence is reflected in Thomas Jefferson's description of the innate rights of man to which "the Laws of Nature and of Nature's God entitle them."

Niagara Falls
The wonder of Niagara Falls symbolized the richness of natural resources and potential for a new nation.

Artistic Romanticism

The romantic viewpoint, a particular way of looking at the relations among God, Nature, and the individual, manifested itself in European literature, music, painting, and sculpture.

In the visual arts, English artists such as J.M.W. Turner (1775–1851) and John Constable (1776–1837) established the visual romantic genre through their landscapes of sea and countryside. Using rich, almost impressionistic colors and tones, they painted with a deep appreciation of the beauties of nature. Turner, for example, explores the interplay between sea and sky with great romantic feeling. Both reflected the contemporary literary and intellectual romantic movements in Europe. Their art conveyed the romantic ideal; that is, they supported the romantic belief that reflections on the beauty of nature could initiate a heightened personal awareness of the senses, and thus approach the spirit of the divine.

In literature, romanticism was dominated by the English poets William Wordsworth (1770–1850) and Samuel Taylor Coleridge (1772–1834). In 1798 Coleridge and Wordsworth published a joint volume of poetry called *Lyrical Ballads* and in so doing launched the English ROMANTIC MOVEMENT. In his *Preface to the Lyrical Ballads,* Wordsworth issues no less than a manifesto on the proper object of poetry in the age of romanticism. There is perhaps no greater concise accounting of romanticism. In this preface, Wordsworth professes all the basic principles of romanticism: He announces the break with tradition (and especially the neoclassical poets of the English Enlightenment, such as Alexander Pope and Samuel Johnson); he exults the power of the romantic poet to give voice to individual feeling; he speaks of the power of nature to show the way of the spirit; he praises the faculty of the imagination to give voice to the subjective experience; and he speaks of the ennobling effects poetry has on the moral condition of humankind.

Wordsworth felt the imagination could take the experiences of everyday men and women and turn them into art. The aim of the *Lyrical* poems was "to choose incidents and situations from common life" and "to throw over them a certain colouring of imagination, whereby ordinary things should be presented to the mind in an unusual aspect." By thus highlighting the ordinary, Wordsworth points to the deeper spirit that lives in all things; the problem, as he sees it, is that human habit has made these wonders too familiar.

Unlike Coleridge, who saw the imagination as the "living power and prime agent of all human perception," Wordsworth felt language and poetry were secondary to the actual experiences of human

&❧ JOHN KEATS, THE SHORT LIFE OF AN IMMORTAL POET &❧
Keats (1795–1821) was perhaps the most promising poet in all of English literature and among the most influential of the Romantics. His death of consumption at the tender age of 25 has always been accompanied by the thought of the greatness he might have achieved had he lived longer. Even so, he managed to pen some of the most famous lines in romantic poetry.

In "Endymion" Keats wrote of the eternal beauty behind nature: "A thing of beauty is a joy forever: its loveliness increases; it will never pass into nothingness." In "To a Nightingale," Keats takes up the theme of immortality again: "Thou wast not born for death, immortal Bird! / No hungry generations tread thee down; / The voice I hear this passing night was heard / In ancient days by emperor and clown." Here, Keats suggests that there is no absolute death in nature: the physical bird and its listener may pass away, but the same scene he describes will be repeated throughout eternity for as long as there are humans to hear and birds to sing.

In his own death Keats became himself a symbol of the romantic poet: His short, brilliant career represented the ephemerality of life, but his poetic achievements revealed also the immortality of art and the poetic spirit. Likening him to the eternal spirit behind nature, Percy Bysshe Shelley (1792–1822) eulogized his friend Keats in his own seminal romantic work, Adonais:

> *He is made one with Nature: there is heard*
> *His voice in all her music; from the moan*
> *Of thunder to the song of night's sweet bird,*
> *He is a presence to be felt and known*
> *In darkness and in light, from herb and stone,*

---

beings: "no words, which his [the poet's] fancy or imagination can suggest, will be to be compared with those which are the emanations of reality and truth." It was the object of poetry to uncover these realities, not to pose as realities themselves.

Wordsworth defends the romantic poet's reliance on personal feelings, "For all good poetry is the spontaneous overflow of powerful feelings." Like Rousseau, Wordsworth claims that human beings have become too distant from their nature. Civilization has stolen their insight into nature away: "the increasing accumulation of men in cities, where the uniformity of their occupations produces a craving for extraordinary incident, which the rapid communication of intelligence hourly gratifies." In other words, the overstimulation of the senses (even in an age without video games) keeps men and women from appreciating the quiet beauty of nature, and with it the opportunity for meditative thought and introspection.

There is pleasure in beauty, Wordsworth writes. And in this sense poetry should gratify the senses. The text should be a pleasure because pleasure "is an acknowledgement of the beauty of the universe." And it is that eternal beauty that the romantic strives to capture in poetry.

In doing so, the poet gives rise to the romantic expression in all human beings. The ultimate aim, for the romantic poet, then, is to elevate his or her reader by revealing their own inner spirits, to show them that even in the most mundane things exists profound beauty. Thus, the reader is "assisted in perceiving that the powers of language are not so limited as he may suppose; and that it is possible for poetry to give other enjoyments, of a purer, more lasting, and more exquisite nature." In this way, Wordsworth believes that the proper aim of all romantic art is to instruct the reader to the "multiplicity and quality of its moral relations" and the higher moral truths that exist in nature.

In the last poem of *Lyrical Ballads,* Wordsworth unveils his great poem "Lines Written a Few Miles Above Tintern Abbey" (1758). In one scene the speaker looks out on the beautiful scene of nature and reflects on the pleasure he feels at both seeing the beauty of nature and the knowledge that in the future, he may draw on its memory at will. It is this power of the imagination to know that things have a life beyond their present reality, which makes the romantic certain of a greater life beyond.

And now, with gleams of half-extinguished thought,
With many recognitions dim and faint,
And somewhat of a sad perplexity,
The picture of the mind revives again:
While here I stand, not only with the sense
Of present pleasure, but with pleasing thoughts
That in this moment there is life and food
For future years.

Romanticism in America

The following chapters chronicle the career of the romantic idea in American literature. All of the principles seen in European romanticism find their way into American thought, especially as these ideas come into the American conscience through the Transcendentalist writers, poets, and thinkers. Romanticism and Transcendentalism had a profound affect on the American character. And yet, one hastens to add, that character was already receptive to such ideas. The exuberance of the American character in the nineteenth century, its optimism, its belief in freedom and individuality, its love affair with nature and the frontier—all combined to provide the most conducive environment for the growth of a romantic philosophy. What follows here is an explanation of how and why romanticism flourished at every level of American society between the years 1800 and 1860, an era as influential as any in the history of American culture.

2. ROMANTICISM AND THE NEW NATION

While Western Europe had always celebrated America as the new world, nineteenth-century Americans began to realize the potential this newness held for achieving a great society. From the Jeffersonian declarations of social equality, to the construction of the railroads, to the innovations in farming and industry technology, to the breathtaking vistas of the Hudson River artists, nearly every facet of American society seemed to reflect, embrace, and even revel in the vibrant novelty of the American experience.

Although romanticism flourished on both sides of the Atlantic in the nineteenth century, the feelings inspired by the American frontier and the formation of a new democratic society endowed America with its own special brand of romanticism. European romanticism tended to be founded on a wish to escape its own history and to start over. America, however, was the embodiment of that wish. Everything was new. Anything was possible. Continually breaking the molds of European traditions, the emergent United States began to place its unique stamp on government, art, philosophy, and literature.

The Political, Social, and Cultural Landscape

Politically, America was in uncharted territory. The American Revolution left a nation of loosely connected states the very real task of creating a workable democratic government. The debate that began between Alexander Hamilton and Thomas Jefferson over the question of states' rights versus a centralized government dominated the political stage for decades, increasing the already deep divisions between the North and South. At the same time, the nation was expanding dramatically to the west of the Appalachian Mountains. After Jefferson's purchase of the Louisiana Territory in 1803, the new nation began its inexorable march to the Pacific, even boldly laying claim, as proclaimed in the Monroe Doctrine of 1823, to the entire Western hemisphere.

Those elected to the presidency in this period reflected America's frontier expansion, if not ambition. Jefferson himself, though a founding father and figure of the Enlightenment, began a movement away from presidents being treated as American monarchs. He paved the way for presidential personalities who symbolized the frontier spirit—indeed, American presidents themselves became romantic heroes. Andrew Jackson, a newly rich frontiersman, ushered in the "age of the common man," which sought to overturn elite political institutions, replacing them—at least in theory—with a more representative democracy. America's romance with the educated frontiersman culminates in the election of Abraham Lincoln to the presidency in 1860.

The Social Landscape

Socially, America was a study in contradictions. On the one hand, the large majority of Americans made their living by farming or by providing products and services to farmers. On the other hand, a growing number began to leave the farms to take jobs in factories and textile mills, especially in the East. As early as 1845, social critics such as Henry David Thoreau (1817–1862) condemned industrial CAPITALISM and the growing mechanization of work.

> I cannot believe that our factory system is the best mode by which men may get clothing   the principal object is, not that mankind may be well and honestly clad, but, unquestionably, that the corporations may be enriched.

One can see in passages such as this the growing ideological clash between the American romantics and economists of the day. To Thoreau's mind, the "progress" of civilization was ruining the frontier spirit, which led him to utter, famously, that the majority of humankind led "lives of quiet desperation." Romantics such as Thoreau believed that humankind could find truth and happiness in nature. The economists of the day disagreed, believing that, rather than preserving nature, it was more important for people and government to advance human commerce.

America's westward expansion increasingly attracted immigrants from all over the world. Land remained plentiful and could be purchased cheaply, jobs were abundant, and America remained a magnet for those seeking political and religious freedom. Thus, America's romance with frontier life continued as ever, and the burgeoning western settlements remained places of hope and promise—at least in the collective romantic imagination—free from traditions, defined by newness and a spirit of exploration.

The Cultural Landscape

Culturally, America also had uneasy ties to tradition. On the one hand, American artists, thinkers, and writers suffered greatly from

❧ A Question of Honor: The Peggy Eaton Affair ❧

Sex scandals have an infamous career in American politics. Historians have characterized the first term of Andrew Jackson's presidency as largely ineffective, partly because Jackson allowed his political opponents to distract him from his agenda as a result of salacious rumors surrounding Margaret "Peggy" Eaton (1796–1879), the wife of his secretary of war.

Mrs. Eaton was by all accounts a beautiful woman, making her an easy target for sexual slander. She was disliked by Floride Calhoun, the wife of Vice President John C. Calhoun, the famed South Carolina pro-slavery advocate. Mrs. Calhoun disapproved of Mrs. Eaton's past. Peggy Eaton was the daughter of a tavern owner, had been married before, and was rumored to have had an affair with Tennessee Senator John Eaton while her husband was at sea. That her husband died at sea only fueled speculation among Washington's proper society. Her subsequent marriage to Senator Eaton did little to improve her social status. Mrs. Eaton was regularly snubbed by the Washington social elite and was not invited to dinner parties and other polite functions.

The slight enraged Jackson, who went to great lengths to defend Mrs. Eaton's honor. For Jackson, the issue was a matter of chivalry. The honor of his friend's wife was at stake, and he was going to defend it at all costs. Jackson was likely oversensitive to the criticisms: His wife, Rachel Donaldson Jackson, had suffered the same kind of character attacks by Jackson's opponents during his presidential bids. That she died just before he took office made him highly sensitive to the treatment that Mrs. Eaton received from Washington society.

He was pilloried by the press and pundits for his support of Peggy Eaton. The scandal eventually tore apart his administration and led to a minor constitutional crisis. In 1831, led by Martin Van Buren, a number of Jackson's cabinet members resigned to help the president put the controversy to rest, creating a rift between Vice President Calhoun and Jackson and leading Jackson to choose Van Buren as his running mate and heir apparent in 1832.

---

what scholar Harold Bloom has called the "anxiety of influence." Europe had a deep and complex cultural history. To ignore this history would be to reject a great deal that was good along with the bad. On the other hand, Americans were deeply suspicious of institutional authority and tradition. At the heart of all of its cultural movements, one can see the palpable pull between the simultaneous needs to invoke tradition on one hand and to rebel against it on the other. American writers wanted forms, themes, and a literary language that were completely new. At the same time, however, they could not help but be influenced by their "Old World" cultural heritage.

It is about this conflict that nineteenth-century American writer Margaret Fuller writes in "American Literature; Its Position in the Present Time, and Prospects for the Future" (1846):

> It does not follow because many books are written by persons born in America that there exists an American literature. Books which imitate or represent the thoughts and life of Europe do not constitute an American literature. Before such can exist, an original idea must animate this nation and fresh currents of life must call into life fresh thoughts along its shores.

For Fuller, America was not yet culturally developed enough to create its own art. Its artists and thinkers were still too enmeshed in European tradition to develop a genuinely American voice—a contention soon to be contradicted by the supremely original poetry of Walt Whitman and Emily Dickinson.

It is also important to note Fuller's use of the imagery of nature and the frontier—she writes of the "fresh currents of life" and "rivers,

➶ THE LEWIS & CLARK ➶ EXPEDITION

On July 4, 1803, news of the purchase of the Louisiana Territory reached the public. Though the size of the United States doubled to encompass 828,000 square miles of land west of the Mississippi River, no one knew for sure what was to be found in these vast lands. On that same day, Thomas Jefferson wrote a letter of credit to Meriwether Lewis to aid in his exploration of the new territory.

It is difficult to imagine today what an adventure into the unknown this expedition was to be. Even the learned and enlightened Jefferson was led to believe from his reading that the West was populated by woolly mammoths and that the land contained active volcanoes and mountains made out of salt. Lewis & Clark managed to dispel many such myths. Following Jefferson's command, the explorers brought back a map to the Pacific Ocean, detailed descriptions of new flora and fauna, and opened a dialogue with dozens of unknown Native American tribes. Upon their return, news of their explorations into the great unknown sparked the collective imagination of the nation.

flowery, luxuriant and impassioned"—to characterize the intellectual differences between the Old World and New. Fuller suggests that the American landscape and its culture are inseparable. The same qualities of the American experience that prevented it from matching the sophistication of European culture also held great promise. Europe, she suggests, has its traditions, but America possesses natural gifts and wonders.

This equation of the American landscape with its national character pervades nineteenth-century American thinking. For the American artist, the tasks were to create a literature that matched the beauty and grandeur of the landscape and to explore how this AESTHETIC could embody the very character of America. Ultimately, this conception of a pristine nature joined with an original American culture became the foundation of American romanticism.

The American Eden

Nineteenth-century America is defined in many ways by the nation's geographical expansion. With the purchase of the Louisiana Territory in 1803, the size of the United States doubled to encompass 828,000 square miles of land west of the Mississippi River, stretching over what are now thirteen states from Louisiana to Minnesota to Wyoming. Expansion continued with the acquisition in 1812 of what is now Florida in 1821, the annexation of Texas (at its request) in 1845, the division (with Great Britain) of the Oregon Territory in 1846, the acquisition of California and New Mexico in 1848 following war with Mexico, and the negotiation of the Gadsden Purchase from Mexico in 1853. In 1800, the American population still clustered along the Atlantic coast. Only one of ten Americans lived beyond the Appalachian Mountains; by 1860, half lived there. As more Americans populated the frontiers, the extent of America's natural gifts began to become widely known.

Nineteenth-century Americans embarked on what can be seen as a love affair with nature. Nature took on deeper spiritual significance, and the American landscape came to be regarded as a new Eden. America as Eden was not a new idea. After all, it was the potential for religious regeneration—inspired by God—that had led the Puritan settlers to the New World in the first place. In *The American Adam,* R.W.B. Lewis suggests that many nineteenth-century American artists made the explicit connection between the biblical Eden and the unspoiled character of America's wilderness.

Perhaps nowhere is the reverence for the American frontier more vivid than in the works of the American landscape artists of the nineteenth century, specifically the Hudson River School. The Hudson

Hudson River School painting
English born immigrant Thomas Cole (1801–1848) founded the Hudson River School, famous for its romantic paintings of the American landscape.

River School is a loose designation for the many landscape artists who lived in the New York City area from the 1820s to the turn of the twentieth century. Their original subject was the natural scenery along the Hudson River and in New England, but these painters also painted landscapes of the American frontier. Thomas Cole (1801–1848) is the acknowledged founder of the movement, along with engraver Asher B. Durand (1796–1886). Cole and Durand influenced a second generation of painters, including Sanford Robinson Gifford (1823–1880), Frederic Edwin Church (1826–1900), John Kensett (1816–1872), Albert Bierstadt (1830–1902), and Worthington Whittredge (1820–1910).

As with other cultural movements in America, the Hudson River School has its roots in European romanticism. English artists such as J.M.W. Turner (1775–1851) and John Constable (1776–1837) had established the visual romantic genre through their critically acclaimed landscapes of the sea and the countryside. Hudson River artists were different from their European counterparts largely because of their subject matter: the majestic beauty of America itself. The American landscapists felt they were eyewitnesses to the great discoveries of American beauty. Throughout the nineteenth century, their paintings were hugely popular around the world, even though many European art critics dismissed their work. With their scenes of vast nature sprawling across large canvases, the Hudson River School painters captured a world enormously large and grand in scale. Set against this wilderness, humankind was small indeed—a part of a larger whole rather than the dominating subject. For example, in works such as Thomas Doughty's *In the Catskills* (1835), Thomas Cole's *The Falls of the Kaaterskill* (1826), or Asher B.

❧ THE LANDSCAPES OF ❧ ALBERT BIERSTADT

Bierstadt (1830–1902) made a small fortune on the sale of his landscapes to patrons all over the world who wanted to own depictions of the natural wonders found throughout America. Bierstadt's masterpiece, **The Rocky Mountains, Lander's Peak (1863),** *resulted from the artist's first trip to the West. In spring 1859, he accompanied a government survey expedition, headed by Colonel Frederick W. Lander, to the Nebraska Territory. When he returned from his travels, the inspired Bierstadt painted a number of large panoramic western landscapes, including* **Lander's Peak.** *This painting is typically Bierstadt: It is large (more than six feet by ten feet), and the scene is peaceful and pastoral: a native American village nestled up against a vast Rocky Mountain landscape, with human figures as an intimate and integrated part of the natural whole. The painting was a popular traveling exhibit, and patrons paid admission to see it.* **Lander's Peak** *was also well-received critically, and it was eventually purchased in 1865 for a then-record sum of $25,000 by an American living in London.*

Durand's *Progress: The Advance of Civilization* (1853), small human characters are dwarfed by their natural settings. Throughout these works, there is an overwhelming sense of divine grandeur contrasted with the smallness of humanity and civilization. If America was the new Eden, its new Adams and Eves were humbled by this second chance in the garden as much as they were elevated by it.

This more complex view of man, God, and nature can be found to be richly documented in the literature of the period. One can best see the development of a fully fledged American romanticism by analyzing the work of two prominent writers, Washington Irving (1783–1859) and James Fenimore Cooper (1789–1851).

Washington Irving and the Sublime

Washington Irving was a prolific and versatile author. He wrote fictional tales, travel sketches, essays, biographies, and national histories—many of which he published in *The Sketch Book of Geoffrey Crayon* (1819–1820). Most of the pieces in the book concern Irving's impressions of England. His subject is often the differences between the English and American character. The success of his narratives of England along with the American tales "The Legend of Sleepy Hollow" and "Rip Van Winkle" made *The Sketch Book* the first American work to gain international literary and popular fame.

By juxtaposing European and American views, Irving presents a case for the differences between English and American romanticism. For Irving, English romanticism was always an idealization of the past, whereas American romanticism lay in its promise for the future. In his preface to the *The Sketch Book,* Irving presents his narrator as a genial, cultivated traveler who fondly describes the picturesque qualities of the English countryside:

> Europe held forth all the charms of storied and poetical association. There were to be seen the masterpieces of art, the refinements of highly cultivated society, the quaint peculiarities of ancient and local custom. My native country was full of youthful promise; Europe was rich in the accumulated treasures of age.

In contrast, the narrator is also drawn to images of the wild, the free, and the PRIMEVAL. These images are based in his sense of the American landscape:

> I visited various parts of my own country . . . [O]n no country have the charms of Nature been more prodigally lavished. Her

mighty lakes, like oceans of liquid silver; her mountains, with their bright aerial tints; her valleys teeming with wild fertility; her tremendous cataracts, thundering in their solitudes; her boundless plains, waving with spontaneous verdure; her broad, deep rivers, rolling in solemn silence to the ocean; her trackless forests where vegetation puts forth all its magnificence; her skies kindling with the magic of summer clouds and glorious sunshine—no, never need an American look beyond his own country for the sublime and the beautiful of natural scenery.

Irving's description of the American landscape shares the same romantic vision of the land held by the Hudson River School painters: mountains, cataracts, boundless plains and forests, all under a magnificent sky. Like these painters, the object of Irving's art is to reveal the SUBLIME in nature.

Indeed, Irving's notion that Americans need not "look beyond [their] own country for the sublime" is a conscious reference to European romanticism, especially to Edmund Burke's famous treatise, *A Philosophical Enquiry into the Origins of Our Ideas of the Sublime and the Beautiful* (1757). Burke suggests that the feeling of the sublime originates in the experience of the terrible greatness of a rugged natural object (such as Niagara Falls), which so astonishes the mind that it fills it with a "delightful horror" or a sense of reverence. Burke's idea, then, is that when a person encounters nature's grandeur, he or she experiences deep emotions, including the sense of reverence that he calls the sublime. This feeling, he suggests, is a sign or symbol of God's infinite, awe-inspiring power. Thus, romantics did not seek an understanding of the divine from books but rather looked to nature for inspiration.

As with the visual artists of his age, Irving locates the sublime not only in nature but also in America itself, a tendency one sees continually in his descriptions of the differences between the nature of England and that of America. In "Rural Life in England," he describes the English garden, subtly contrasting it with the "sublime prospects" of the American wild:

A great part of the island is rather level, and would be monotonous, were it not for the charms of culture; but it is studded and gemmed, as it were, with castles and palaces, and embroidered with parks and gardens. It does not abound in grand and sublime prospects, but rather in little home scenes of rural repose and sheltered quiet.

ঌ Rip Van Winkle ঌ

Washington Irving's "Rip Van Winkle" (1819) is one of the best-known literary folktales of American literature. Drawn from Germanic folklore, Irving's tale applies an American setting to the tale of a man who falls asleep only to reawaken 20 years later to find everything changed.

> *I was myself last night, but I fell asleep on the mountain, and they've changed my gun, and every thing's changed, and I'm changed, and I can't tell what's my name, or who I am.*

The greater part of the story is spent developing the character of Rip's life before his deep sleep. An idler and romantic, Rip spends his days avoiding the nagging of his shrewish wife, fishing, playing with the town children, and otherwise avoiding his domestic duties of family and on the farm. In a scene that portrays (if not satirizes) the popular clubs of romantic philosophers in his day, Irving describes the idle conversations of Rip and his circle of friends:

> *a kind of perpetual club of the sages, philosophers, and other idle personages of the village, [who] used to sit in the shade, of a long lazy summer's day, talking listlessly over village gossip, or telling endless sleepy stories about nothing.*

One day while avoiding his shrewish wife's recriminations, Rip happens upon the place of his long rest. Irving describes a romantic scene of nature worthy of the Hudson River School painters: "He saw at a distance the lordly Hudson, far, far below him, moving on its silent but majestic course."

Rip's reawakening quickly evolves into a happy ending, and his. Rip's kind fate offers up a surprising moral twist to the story: whereas such fables typically reward the industrious individual, the lazy Rip, "one of those happy mortals, of foolish, well-oiled dispositions," finds his niche among the more enlightened Americans of the future. And so, the idle traveler, lover of nature and philosophical conversation, assumes a home in "modern" America, the triumph of the romantic individual complete.

Washington Irving affirms the "romantic revolution" in American culture in one other respect: He associates Native Americans with the pristine beauty of American nature. In *Astoria* (1836), his narrative history of the great Northwest Fur Company, Irving celebrates the romantic chivalry of the Native Americans. Indeed, he thought of Native Americans as a heroic people who partook of the grandeur of the American landscape. In "Traits of Indian Character" (1819), Irving writes:

> There is something in the character and habits of the North American savage, taken in connection with the scenery over which he is accustomed to range, its vast lakes, boundless forests, majestic rivers, and trackless plains, that is, to my mind, wonderfully striking and sublime. He is formed for the wilderness, as the Arab is for the desert. His nature is stern, simple, and enduring, fitted to grapple with difficulties and to support privations.

Notwithstanding his optimism about the American future, Irving also saw the threats to the romantic ideal. He realized that as the United States expanded over the North American continent, the wild landscape would be profoundly altered. Irving often wrote of the devastation of the Native American cultures in a mournful tone. With the disappearance of Native American tribes, an inspiring and noble way of being would forever be lost to the world. In common with the romantics who were to follow him, Irving associated the progress of "civilization" with the loss of spiritual vitality.

James Fenimore Cooper and the American Character

No writer did more to consolidate the romantic strain in the American character than James Fenimore Cooper. Cooper recognized early in his literary career that the true national literature of the United States must be reflective of the political culture of the young republic. The American writer needed to bring to light those unique characteristics that made the Americans a real national people. The problem, as Cooper saw it in his *Notions of the Americans* (1828), was that the United States lacked the historical experience and the social customs and manners that could be found in European art. In particular, the United States was devoid of the legends, myths, and folklore that were the proper objects for the romancer.

Cooper first sought to dignify the American experience by exploiting the literary potential of the American West. Cooper wrote eight

Last of the Mohicans
James Fenimore Cooper's (1789–1851) *Last of the Mohicans* dramatized the
conflict between nature and civilization on the American frontier.

romances of the western frontier, but by far the most important are the five works which constitute the Leatherstocking series: *The Pioneers* (1823), *The Last of the Mohicans* (1826), *The Prairie* (1827), *The Pathfinder* (1840), and *The Deerslayer* (1841). Considered as a whole, the five tales chronicle the life and times of the frontier scout, hunter, and trapper, Natty Bumpo. Natty Bumpo is also known as "Leatherstocking," "Pathfinder," "Deerslayer," and "Hawkeye," in accordance with his wilderness skills and martial prowess.

In terms of the development of American romanticism, the Leatherstocking series made three vital contributions: It laid the foundation for the heroic myth of the essential American as the westerner who lives close to nature; it firmly consolidated the mythic notion of the Native American as a child of nature; and, finally, it helped to establish the sublime western landscape (of prairies, forests, and mountains) as the preeminent American setting, the place where the uniqueness of the American national character was most easily seen.

Natty Bumpo is an illiterate backwoodsman who is singularly adept with his gun. He has lived among the Indians, and is well-versed in their ways, but he insists on his white racial identity and his sense of personal honor. Cooper modeled his character partly on the legendary folk hero Daniel Boone (1734–1820) and partly on the romantic myth of the primitive natural man, whose simple honesty, moral insight, and code of chivalry demonstrates a harmonious spiritual relationship to the sensible world. Natty Bumpo has all the virtues of the Indians and none of their vices. He stands at odds with the moral corruptions and social absurdities that, for Cooper, are all too characteristic of civilized society. Throughout the Leatherstocking series, Cooper contrasts the organic, spontaneous, and generous qualities of Natty with the mechanical, contrived, and mean-spirited qualities of overcivilized people—the lawyers, professors, merchants, landholders, and greedy settlers who are at the forefront of the westward moving frontier.

Cooper believed that the Native American was the romantic antique type of the American continent, just as the Greeks were the antique types of the Old World. Similar to Rousseau's conception of the primitive, Native Americans represented a pure and natural race that lived in accordance with nature. Like Irving, Cooper lamented the loss of this society, which seemed at times to be an improvement over the often-treacherous world of white civilization. Natty Bumpo's Indian friend Uncas, the last of the Mohicans, is an example of this noble ideal. Cooper describes Uncas as "graceful and unrestrained in the attitudes and movements of nature." His outwardly "rich natural gifts" are symbolic of his inward good and noble character.

Cooper's treatment of landscape closely parallels the romantic vision of the Hudson River School. In his 1835 "Essay on American Scenery," Thomas Cole observed that "the wilderness is yet a fitting place to speak of God." Cooper shared this assumption. Natty Bumpo will sometimes speak of nature in these pantheistic terms. For example, in *The Prairie,* the sublimity of the wilderness highlights the darker aspects of civilization, particularly its ecological destructiveness, which Natty holds to be a mortal sin against God's Nature.

The five romances of the Leatherstocking series might be considered a national epic in prose. Their most fundamental tendency is the translation of history into myth. The characters and the settings are larger-than-life symbols of the meaning of the American experience. In these mythic types, Cooper dramatizes the social and political contradictions of the frontier. Ultimately, he defines the American character as resting somewhere between civilization and the wilderness.

As we have seen, the American landscape indeed, nature it self–plays a crucial role in defining American romanticism. It becomes further ingrained in the American consciousness as it is developed into the philosophical system of the Transcendentalists.

3. TRANSCENDENTALISM

Nothing seemed to deter America's growth in the nineteenth century. Geographically, the nation was pushing the frontiers to the Pacific; politically, it was finding its identity as a democratic government divided into executive, judicial, and legislative branches; socially, it was in a fervent state of development, constantly creating and setting up new communities within its ever-expanding boundaries. Such growth and advancement imbued Americans with a collective sense of optimism and belief in progress. Americans knew they had a special place in history, and that feeling pervaded everything they thought, did, or believed.

It is in this environment that a new American philosophy would take root: Transcendentalism. As much religion as philosophy, Transcendentalism provided a system of beliefs that adequately reflected the prevailing thoughts and opinions of Americans. The Transcendentalist movement created a romantic philosophy that would become a rallying point for America's greatest thinkers, artists, and poets, who were already intent upon finding a way to express the essential spirit of the American experience.

Historical Trends of the Early Nineteenth Century

The framers of the U.S. Constitution in 1787 had boldly crafted a new experiment on the world's political stage. In 1800, when the REPUBLICANS wrested control of the federal government from the FEDERALISTS, it was not yet clear whether government based on the consent of the governed with powers divided between the central and state levels could survive. The political faith that "all men are created equal," as expressed in the Declaration of Independence, was only an ideal.

Thomas Jefferson pointed the nation toward the lodestar of social equality by embracing the slogan, "Equal opportunity for all and special privileges for none." His reasoning was that those with wealth did not deserve help, and everybody else would not need it if they had an open field and a fair chance. Jefferson helped translate the slogan into reality by acquiring the LOUISIANA PURCHASE, which doubled the size of the United States and opened for settlement the wonderfully rich farmland west of the Mississippi. By so doing, he created exactly the opportunity he thought all Americans would need.

During the era associated with the presidency of Andrew Jackson (1829–1837) the slogan largely became reality. Between Jefferson and Jackson the frontier expansion and population growth were transforming American society. After the WAR OF 1812, Carolinians and Georgians packed up wagons, hitched farm animals behind them, and made their way southwestward into territories soon to become Alabama, Mississippi, and Louisiana; Virginians trekked across the Appalachians into Tennessee and Kentucky; New Englanders on rafts and flat boats floated down the Ohio River toward Ohio, Indiana, and Illinois.

As these territories became states, they chose not to limit the right to vote to property owners (as had the seaboard states) but extended it to all free adult males. Though critics were dismayed that "every biped of the forest" could vote, they were correct in recognizing that change was afoot. By the 1820s not only could more people vote but also more people were interested in participating in the political process. Early on, the mechanism through which politics had worked was deference; social inferiors deferred to their betters and trusted them to choose deserving or able leaders. By the 1820s popular appeal was replacing deference. And what appealed to voters was the self-made man, which Andrew Jackson symbolized.

🐦 ANDREW JACKSON, 🐦 SELF-MADE MAN

Andrew Jackson's family owned a small farm along the Carolina piedmont. Orphaned during the American Revolution while in his middle teens, Jackson sought opportunity on the Tennessee frontier where he soon displayed considerable skill in making his own way. He practiced law (without formal training), became a judge for a time, acquired land, bought slaves, operated a plantation, and became a national hero during the War of 1812 after devising the daring strategy that enabled a motley assortment of Americans in New Orleans to trounce British forces fresh from campaigns against Napoleon.

Jackson was different from presidents before him. While earlier ones had come from the Atlantic seaboard, Jackson lived in the New West (Tennessee) when he was elected. He was the first president since George Washington to have had no college education. And he owed his election to no geographic interest or social group; he had been raised by ordinary people who hoped to do as extraordinarily well as he had done.

The policies adopted while Jackson was president, even decisions of the Supreme Court, reflected this changed America by continually valuing energy, enterprise, and personal achievement. Economically, LAISSEZ-FAIRE capitalism reigned. In fact, a foreign visitor commented that America was like a giant workshop over which was emblazoned a sign, declaring "No Admission Here Except on

Business." This emphasis on business, on growing personal wealth and getting ahead, became the underpinning for what most Americans believed was the ideal democratic society.

Cities grew in size. In 1800 there were only two with a population greater than 50,000; by 1860 there were sixteen (and eight of them exceeded 100,000). As the population scattered, the number of states increased—from 16 in 1800 to 33 in 1860. Population also shifted northward. In 1800 the distribution was roughly equal, North and South; by 1860 the ratio was more than 2:1 (22 million in the North to nine million in the South, including 3.5 million persons of color—not all slaves).

The growth and expansion in the first half of nineteenth-century America gave the nation a firm belief in its own progress. The political and economic climate that created self-made successes out of men like Andrew Jackson instilled the populace with faith in the power of the individual to rise above his or her own circumstances and fashion his or her own place in the world. This collective sense of rising above, both on a cultural and individual level, created fertile ground for an optimistic, if not idealistic, American philosophy to take hold. It is this environment in which a small group of New Englanders would sow the seeds of Transcendentalism.

The Transcendental Club and a Little Beyond

In 1836, in Concord, Massachusetts, a group of intellectuals convened to discuss the state of American thought, philosophy, art, education, and religion. The group met roughly over a four-year period and most often at the home of Ralph Waldo Emerson (1803–1882), a former Unitarian minister who had resigned his post in order that he might think freely, and not be bound by certain dogmas.

Among the group members were the Unitarian ministers Frederic Henry Hedge (1805–1890), William Ellery Channing (1780–1842), Theodore Parker (1810–1860), and George Ripley (1802–1880); the philosopher and educator Amos Bronson Alcott (1799–1888); and the poet Jones Very (1813–1880). Henry David Thoreau (1817–1862) regularly attended meetings, as did Margaret Fuller (1810–1850). Occasional members included the journalist Orestes Brownson (1803–1876) and the novelist Nathaniel Hawthorne (1804–1864). It was a motley group, and individual members disagreed on many issues. Nonetheless, all members shared a commitment to advancing the present state of philosophy, religion, and literature in America. Because of their interest in the ideas of Kant,

❧ TRANSCENDENTALISM AND UNITARIANISM ❧

Many Transcendentalists were closely connected to the Unitarian Church. Unitarianism grew in part as rejection of CALVINISM, the religion of the Puritans. The French theologian John Calvin (1509–1564) had argued that all people were born in sin, that God's grace fell on the predestined, and that the rest would be damned. This became an essential doctrine of the Puritans. The old Calvinistic notion of predestination was set aside by the Unitarian church, which believed that salvation should be available to all. They argued that if all humans are made in "likeness to God," then all humans were potentially good and all might be perfected.

The transition from Unitarianism to Transcendentalism owed much to the mind of William Ellery Channing (1780–1842). In his lecture "Self Culture," Channing suggests that greatness of God is common to all men:

> *Let us not disparage that nature which is common to all men; for no thought can measure its grandeur. It is the image of God, the image even of his infinity, for no limits can be set to its unfolding. He who possesses the divine powers of the soul is a great being, be his place what it may. You may clothe him with rags, may immure him in a dungeon, may chain him to slavish tasks. But he is still great.*

Channing's romantic theology stated that all human beings could find the divine spirit within themselves. Emerson repeatedly emphasized this theme throughout his writings. He often denied the Calvinist notion that God was an awful spiritual presence who was far removed from the ordinary human being. He counseled people to find God in all things.

---

which were "transcendent," or focusing on matters beyond the material world and sense perceptions, the group came to be known as the Transcendental Club.

Ralph Waldo Emerson wrote in his journal on October 6, 1836, "Transcendentalism means, says our accomplished Mrs. B. [Almira Penningman Barlow] with a wave of her hand, *A little beyond*."

Emerson was half in jest here, because in one sense Transcendentalism was *a great leap beyond* the ordinary material world. It saw the entire physical universe as only a representation of a higher spiritual world. "Nature," wrote Emerson, "is the symbol of the spirit."

Yet, in another sense, Transcendentalism was truly a matter of going *a little beyond*. Transcendentalists assumed that the ultimate truth of the spiritual nature of the universe was readily at hand—natural and accessible to every human being.

According to the Transcendentalist, a farmer at work in the corn fields, a poet thinking through the logic of a certain metaphor, a scientist bent on discovering the natural cause behind the diversity of song birds, and a reformer committed to struggling against social injustices—all these individuals are involved in revealing the "higher laws" of the world that cannot be perceived by the senses. This Transcendent realm is both near and far: it seems far when we lose sight of ourselves as spiritual beings and go about our daily business in the manner of unthinking animals or machines; but it is understood to be very near to us the moment we see the world and ourselves on a more philosophical, aesthetic, or moral level. In other words, when we observe the spirit beyond things and sense perception, we transcend ourselves and participate in that higher reality. In this way, we live in the world as God intended.

Perhaps the best way to understand Transcendentalism is that it also went a little beyond European Romanticism, causing many to define the transcendental movement as American Romanticism. Like European Romanticism, Transcendentalism shares many of the same characteristic attitudes: a deep appreciation of nature; a preference of emotion over reason; a belief in the self and the potential of the individual; a predilection for the artist in particular and the creative spirit in general; and a distrust of classical forms and traditions.

The difference is that Transcendentalism arose out of the crucible of the American experience. Transcendentalism shared the same values as nineteenth-century Americans, especially in its optimism, faith in the individual, and belief in democracy. A central tenet of Transcendentalism was the conviction that human beings could elevate themselves beyond their baser animal instincts, attain a higher consciousness, and take part in the spirit of the divine. Transcendentalism was also democratic in its principles. Transcendentalists believed that all people were equal in the eyes of God, and all had sufficient spiritual power to intuit God in their daily lives. Until 1860, there was no reason for the collective body of Americans to disbelieve such higher views of humankind. America was making such great progress economically, politically, technologically, culturally that it seemed to many that the direction and destiny of America was obviously toward a higher evolution of humankind.

Although individual Transcendentalists differed greatly on a great number of subjects, a clear picture of the essential character of

Transcendentalism can be found in an examination of two of its most prominent proponents, Ralph Waldo Emerson (1803–1882) and Henry David Thoreau (1817–1862).

Emerson's *Nature* and "Self-Reliance"

In his essay, "Circles," Emerson observes that when God lets loose a great thinker on this planet, "then all things are at risk." The great thinker is what Emerson called a "representative man," an individual who manages to embody in his own person a universal aspect of spirit. Such has been Emerson's influence on American culture that he himself is widely regarded as a representative man. One reason for Emerson's popularity was that he was not only an author but also an extremely active and successful speaker, delivering about 1,500 lectures during his career. He traveled throughout the country, venturing as far West as San Francisco. Emerson's lectures were the bases for many of his essays. The former Unitarian minister preached on themes such as self-reliance, self-knowledge, and nonconformity.

Emerson spoke eloquently about the spiritual matters that were troubling Americans in the nineteenth century. What was the American spirit? How was it different than that of Europe? As humans began to populate and clear the frontiers, what was the proper relation between humankind and nature? How was belief in the spirit supposed to translate to government, especially to social reform in matters such as slavery? Emerson's works and lectures provided answers to a wide audience—many of whom were not Transcendentalists—

ADVANCEMENTS IN TRANSPORTATION TECHNOLOGY

When the nineteenth century opened, people still were moving from one place to another in the same way their ancestors had done for thousands of years—on foot, horseback, or animal-drawn vehicle. All that was about to change—and to change dramatically. The construction of turnpikes was the first innovation, beginning privately in Pennsylvania and then becoming public with the National Road. The era of canal building began in 1817 with the construction of the Erie Canal. Completed in 1825 it became the major artery connecting eastern and western sections of the United States, transforming New York City into a metropolis by 1860.

After cities to the south made unsuccessful attempts at canal building, they turned to another innovation from England, the railway. The development of the railroads—and the application of the steam engine to water travel—revolutionized movement of people and goods in the United States. By train a person could travel farther in an hour than had been possible previously by canal in an entire day. The ratio between distance and travel time in the United States declined so dramatically that it was easier in 1860 to travel across the entire continent than it had been to reach Lake Michigan from New York City in 1800. In fact, one could travel to Chicago from New York City in less than two days in 1860; in 1800, the trip stretched through six weeks!

which was hungry for an American philosophy that related to their everyday experiences.

Emerson's romantic philosophy is most clearly seen in his work, *Nature* (1836). In *Nature,* Emerson describes a world in which nearly everything in it is a symbol of the spirit. For Emerson, nature is the material world, everything that exists outside the self. This world is one-half, a cover over a greater realm, the spirit or Soul. The problem with humankind, however, is that it continually focuses on the appearance of nature, rarely peering into its essence.

> To speak truly, few adult persons can see nature. Most persons do not see the sun. At least they have a very superficial seeing. The sun illuminates only the eye of the man, but shines into the eye and the heart of the child. The lover of nature is he whose inward and outward senses are still truly adjusted to each other; who has retained the spirit of infancy even into the era of manhood.

Emerson alludes to the "childlike" appreciation of nature intentionally, for he believes that the appreciation of nature is innate in human beings, but lost over time as people go about the business of living (which he defines as "COMMODITY").

The higher purposes of nature lay in Beauty. It is the artist who can convey, indeed remind, all people of their ability to see the beauty inherent in all things. The creation of beauty, says Emerson, is art; beauty leads men to virtue and heroism. But ultimately beauty brings humans to God:

> The world thus exists to the soul to satisfy the desire of beauty. This element I call an ultimate end. No reason can be asked or given why the soul seeks beauty. Beauty, in its largest and profoundest sense, is one expression for the universe. God is the all-fair. Truth, and goodness, and beauty, are but different faces of the same All.

For Emerson, all of nature leads to the same lesson, namely that "Nature is the symbol of spirit." Once people begin looking for the spirit that lives within the world, it is then that they become PANTHE- ISTS, able to see God in everything.

In a world in which everything is spirit and everything is one with God, the question arises, what, then, is MY role in this world? It is this question that Emerson takes up in perhaps his most famous essay, "Self-Reliance" (1841). Emerson is as certain of an inner goodness in all human beings as he is of the goodness of nature. The problem, however, is that human beings lose sight of this quality, largely because of the influence of the mass of humanity. Institutional thought, tired traditions, even religion make people unthinking and overly cautious, so worried about what others think that they cannot think on their own. This tendency to go about life safely and without conflict renders people mediocre, a condition which Emerson warns against in his famous maxim: "A foolish consistency is the hobgoblin of little minds."

For Emerson, the world at large is always at odds with the individual, which is why he counsels everyone to be a NONCONFORMIST. Emerson believed that people were too ready to conform to the values of others, that they suppressed themselves as particular individuals. "Insist on yourself; never imitate," writes Emerson, for "imitation is suicide." Emerson felt that human individuality was a wondrous "Spiritual fact," that God meant for us to behave like individuals because each of us is wholly unique.

Emerson believed that to live in accord with spiritual reality was perhaps the most difficult thing in the world. Just as in orthodox Christianity grace is not easily achieved but must be won over and over in the face of the daily temptation to sin, so in Emerson's system one does not become a Transcendentalist without serious effort. Most people, without actually realizing that they are accepting a philosophical system, are materialists; they believe that matter has more reality than spirit. The end result is that people treat themselves and others as mere *physical things*. To recover one's *spiritual being,* one must practice "self-reliance"; that is, one has to renounce the ordinary beliefs and customs that most people readily accept and look for truth within the self.

Thoreau's Theory of Living

Henry David Thoreau (1817–1862) was a former Harvard student from Concord, Massachusetts. He worked in a number of professions—as a teacher, a land surveyor, and a laborer (and sometime inventor) in his father's pencil factory. In 1845, wanting to write his first book, he ventured off to the woods and built a cabin near Walden Pond on a parcel of land owned by Emerson. He later wrote about his experiences in *Walden, or Life in the Woods* (1854), which has become the definitive text of Transcendentalism and one of the most famous works in American literature.

Thoreau begins *Walden* by addressing his audience in the first person, explaining: "I should not talk so much about myself if there were any body else whom I knew as well. Unfortunately, I am confined to this theme by the narrowness of my experience." Throughout this first chapter, "Economy," Thoreau presents the reader with this "I," who surveys the world he lives in and explains plainly what he thinks is wrong with it. There are, then, two subjects always present in *Walden*: (1) the state of living as practiced by people in Thoreau's world; and (2) the author himself. Thoreau gives a startling panorama of his world, providing great insight into how people went about the business of living in New England in the 1840s. At the same time, the author reveals glimpses of an extraordinary individual, a 28-year-old young man who is intelligent, discontented, and searching for a better way to live.

The thesis of "Economy" is contained in Thoreau's famous declaration: "The mass of men live lives of quiet desperation." Thoreau proves his argument—in his roundabout prose—by pointing to the bare necessities of life and then showing how unnecessarily hard humankind has made it to acquire them. "It is not necessary," Thoreau writes, "that a man should earn his living by the sweat of his brow, unless he sweats easier than I do." To show how much more humankind adds to his life's' burdens, Thoreau addresses the three basic necessities of food, shelter, and clothing. He shows (in itemized grocery lists, no less) that food staples could be gotten cheaply, while most else could be grown in the earth. "I learned from my two years' experience that it would cost incredibly little trouble to obtain one's necessary food, even in this latitude; that a man may use as simple a diet as the animals, and yet retain health and strength." Shelter and clothing, too, could be built and stitched with one's own hands. All necessities could be more easily attained than by the way "civilized"

❧ TRANSCENDENTALISM ❧ AND ASIAN RELIGIONS

Confucian, Hindu, and Buddhist themes can be found throughout the writings of the Transcendentalists. Emerson and Thoreau were familiar with English translations of the Hindu Vedas or scriptures known as **The Upanishads.** *Emerson thought that "the Oriental Mind" was intrinsically spiritual because it had always tended to comprehensiveness. He regarded Hinduism and Buddhism as anticipations of the ideal Transcendentalism. Emerson was intrigued by the doctrine of perpetual reincarnation, which holds that a spirit never dies but merely changes forms. Emerson saw the same in Nature, which he believed to be circular and eternal.*

Both Emerson and Thoreau shared with the Buddhists the belief that the world is given over to maya or illusion: most people are unaware of what it really means to be human. Like the Buddhists, Emerson and Thoreau believed in renouncing the ego (or physical self) for the true spiritual self. Buddhists believe that physical desires—because they are ephemeral—lead to pain and suffering. The Buddhist doctrine of the futility of sensual, earthly pleasures underpins a great deal of the argument of Thoreau's **Walden.**

Walden Pond
A practice started by Bronson Alcott (1799–1888), visitors to Walden Pond, near Lincoln and Concord, Massachusetts, place stones on a rock pile to memorialize the site where Thoreau lived out his Transcendental experiment.

human beings went about it. Throughout, Thoreau demonstrates the absurdity of "modern" life. "Most of the luxuries," he writes, "and many of the so called comforts of life, are not only not indispensable, but positive hinderances to the elevation of mankind."

There is sharp contrast in the prose and subject matter of the second chapter of *Walden*, "Where I Lived and What I Lived For." Having given the reader a brief glimpse into the real world, he turns the discussion to the ideal world, symbolized by Walden Pond itself.

> For the first week, whenever I looked out on the pond it impressed me like a tarn high up on the side of a mountain, its bottom far above the surface of other lakes, and, as the sun arose, I saw it throwing off its nightly clothing of mist, and here and there, by degrees, its soft ripples or its smooth reflecting surface was revealed, while the mists, like ghosts, were stealthily withdrawing in every direction into the woods, as at the breaking up of some nocturnal conventicle. The very dew seemed to hang upon the trees later into the day than usual, as on the sides of mountains.

This romantic description of nature begins a much more introspective voyage into the self. Thoreau delves into the reasons for his experiment in the woods, reasons which are deeply personal. Today, the site of Thoreau's humble cabin on Walden Pond is marked by this passage: "I went to the woods because I wished to live deliberately, to front only the essential facts of life, and see if I could not learn what it had to teach, and not, when I came to die, discover that I had not lived." Death is very much on Thoreau's mind. In 1842, his brother John cut himself while shaving and subsequently died of lockjaw. The untimely death troubled Thoreau, and during his stay at Walden Pond he wrote *A Week on the Concord and Merrimack Rivers* (1849), a book about a river expedition that he and his brother once took. The fragility of life was ever on Thoreau's mind, and one of the reasons he cites for his experiment, is that he "wanted to live deep and suck out all the marrow of life, to live so sturdily and Spartan-like as to put to rout all that was not life." In short, Thoreau's trip to Walden taught him to seize the day, to make every moment of every day count.

The beauty of nature reminds Thoreau to live life to the highest principles. In nature, Thoreau finds instructions for living life according to the simplest and most basic terms. But more importantly, the beauty that he perceives in nature reminds him of the possibility of living life according to a higher reality. It is this lesson learned during his forays into the woods that he offers to his readers:

> We must learn to reawaken and keep ourselves awake, not by mechanical aids, but by an infinite expectation of the dawn, which does not forsake us in our soundest sleep. I know of no more encouraging fact than the unquestionable ability of man to elevate his life by a conscious endeavor.

These two chapters of *Walden* highlight key aspects of Transcendentalism. Thoreau's "economical" viewpoint of the world calls into question society's concern for things that do not matter. In "Economy," we can see how Transcendentalism clashed with economic principles of the day. For the Transcendentalists, capitalism was inherently materialistic, and materialism was inherently wrong. Mankind must see the higher reality behind things, not worship the things themselves. In "What I Lived For," we see the other side of Transcendentalism, the serious quest for finding the self and the ability of nature to facilitate that journey.

In the end, it might be said that Emerson gave Transcendentalism its philosophy. Thoreau, for his part, turned that philosophy into a practical theory of living.

4. THE LITERATURE OF ROMANTIC REFORM

Many historians have come to see the period between 1830 and 1860 as a "Search for Heaven on Earth." A social reform effort, this widespread quest reflected the influence of the Transcendentalists and a belief in the "perfectibility" of human beings. Many thoughtful people, especially the culturally elite, had become convinced that human beings would approach perfection as the circumstances of their lives improved. Remove artificial barriers, the argument went, and individuals would be able to "make real" their potential.

Reform Movements of Nineteenth-Century America

The artificial barriers that reformers noticed cut across the fabric of society: ignorance, abuse of alcohol, imprisoning the insane in jails, diet, and slavery. Literacy was limited. Learning was considered a private responsibility, mainly of the family or of the church. By the 1830s a ground swell of support for free schools began to emerge in Massachusetts under the leadership of Horace Mann (1796–1859). By 1860 the principle of publicly supported free schools had been adopted in states outside the South, and grammar schools were being established.

Alcohol consumption was reaching levels higher than ever before—or since—in American experience. There was concern that many with limited income, especially unskilled laborers, were wasting their meager resources on strong drink, and, as a result, neglecting their families. Efforts focused on persuading them to "take the pledge"—not to abstain, but simply to drink in moderation. This campaign was remarkably successful, bringing about dramatic reduction in per capita alcohol consumption.

Even diet became a target for reform, and the slogan "You are what you eat" was often repeated. A lingering reminder of the reformists' efforts is the graham cracker, named for the person who popularized it on the now widely accepted conviction that whole grain was good for people.

In addition, initial efforts on behalf of women's rights were made during this period. In 1848, the first women's rights convention gathered in Seneca Falls, New York. One proposal that was adopted there modified the Declaration of Independence and expanded it. To the phrase, "We declare these truths to be self-evident: that all men are created equal," the convention added (after all men) "and all women." They declined, however, to advocate for the right to vote for women. When this was suggested, one Quakeress chided, "Thee will make us look ridiculous!"

The Antislavery Movement

The antislavery movement was the most enduring of the reform efforts. Eventually it eclipsed all the others, draining off support from them and taking on the proportions of a crusade. It divided Americans into opposing camps. The antislavery movement began gradually, led by persons with African ancestry. By the 1830s white abolitionists became active, including William Lloyd Garrison (1805–1879), Theodore Weld (1803–1895), the Grimke sisters (Sarah, 1792–1873, and Angelina, 1805–1879), Wendell Phillips (1811–1884), and Harriet Beecher Stowe (1811–1896). Garrison, a strident opponent of slavery, founded the New England Antislavery Society (1832) followed by the American Antislavery Society (1833). By 1840 there were 2,000 local societies with 200,000 members. Others also provided leadership. Though not an organizer, Stowe greatly stimulated the growth of antislavery sentiment. Her novel, *Uncle Tom's Cabin,* became the most powerful literary weapon in the abolitionists' assault.

✿ INSANE ASYLUMS ✿

A cause that attracted attention in the 1840s was treatment of the insane. Dorothea Dix (1802–1887), during a tour of jails in the Northeast, was appalled to find many persons there who were obviously deranged. She devoted the rest of her life to the creation of separate facilities for the mentally ill, called insane asylums, where attempts would be made to treat them, not simply to detain them.

From 1848 to 1854, Dix lobbied the federal government to create a national mental health institute. Although it won support in Congress, it was vetoed by President Franklin Pierce for political reasons. During the Civil War, Dix worked to set up field hospitals and training facilities for nurses. After the war, she was disheartened to find that conditions for the mentally ill had deteriorated once again. Although the results of her lifelong reform efforts did not live up to her expectations, Dix set the stage for vast improvements in the next century.

Other opponents had cited statistics about slaves and their families, using a rational approach. Stowe, however, presented slaves as well as slaveholders as flesh and blood individuals, creating emotional appeal. Furthermore, she avoided demonizing slaveholders by attacking the institution of slavery, contending that it brutalized both master and slave. When published in 1852, 300,000 copies of the book were sold; when later dramatized as a play, countless others saw it and came away disapproving of slavery.

Opponents of slavery embraced several courses of action against it, both official and personal. The official action included urging states to refrain from cooperation with the federal government in enforcing the 1793 FUGITIVE SLAVE LAW, urging the federal government to abolish slavery in Washington, D.C., and in the territories, and urging the federal government to ban interstate slave trade. The personal action included assisting runaway slaves and setting up educational facilities for free persons of color.

Reaction to the antislavery movement was divided, North and South. In the North some were sympathetic, others hostile; in the South the white population was overwhelmingly united in hostility to anything that threatened their peculiar institution (as they called slavery). In fact, southerners created an elaborate defense of slavery, shifting their description of it in the 1830s from a necessary evil to a positive good. John C. Calhoun (1782–1850) played a major role in the defense of slavery, as did George Fitzhugh (1806–1881) of Virginia.

Slavery was tacitly accepted in the Constitution of 1787, but in that same year the Confederation Congress took a small step toward corralling it. The Congress adopted the Northwest Ordinance of 1787, providing an orderly progression toward statehood for what historians now call the Old Northwest. It also planned for the support of education, and it prohibited slavery in the Old Northwest. (Wisconsin became one of these states.) Early on, the expansion of slavery became a hot-button issue. For example, when Missouri sought admission as a slave state, approval was delayed until the MISSOURI COMPROMISE of 1820 was enacted. This compromise allowed Missouri to be admitted as a slave state, while at

GEORGE RIPLEY AND BROOK FARM

Transcendentalists not only lent their substantial intellects to romantic social reform movements but they also attempted to live their ideas by creating their own ideal communities. In 1841 the former Unitarian minister George Ripley (1802–1880) and other Transcendentalists established the cooperative community of Brook Farm on a 175-acre farm in West Roxbury, Massachusetts. The farm was envisaged as a sort of Transcendentalist model community, which might serve as both a philosophic and economic example to other Americans.

The overall aim of the COMMUNE *was "to prepare a society of liberal, intelligent, and cultivated persons, whose relations with each other would permit a more simple and wholesome life." The members voluntarily worked the farm, working typically 8- to 10-hour days. The rest of the time was spent in pleasurable social activities: dancing, music, plays, discussions, parties, and picnics. The destruction by fire of the farm's central building led to such significant financial losses for the group that they were forced to abandon the experiment. Nathaniel Hawthorne's novel,* **The Blithedale Romance** *(1852), is a wry fictional treatment of the history of Brook Farm.*

the same time admitting Maine as a free state, thus retaining the balance of slave to free states. The Missouri Compromise also prohibited the spread of slavery in the rest of the Louisiana territory. The KANSAS-NEBRASKA ACT OF 1854, however, allowed Kansas residents themselves to accept or reject slavery—thereby repealing the Missouri Compromise. In the wake of the Kansas-Nebraska Act, a new, one-issue party opposed to the spread of slavery was formed: the Republican Party. This led to the eventual demise of the WHIG PARTY, as many of its members joined the new organization.

The drift toward disunion became a slide. With the raid of John Brown on Harper's Ferry in 1859, which intended to arm slaves and foment a widespread uprising against slaveholders, the United States faced the abyss of disunion. Though some condemned Brown (who was hanged) as a criminal, others, such as Emerson, hailed him as a saint. Southern leaders, hearing Emerson, decided to secede from the union if a Republican should ever be elected to the presidency. Less than a month after Lincoln's election, the South, led by South Carolina, made good on its threat. Morally divided by the bitter debate over slavery, the United States was splintered by the spring of 1861.

Transcendentalism and the Reform Movements

At the core of Transcendentalism was the conviction that human beings could rise above their animal instincts and live according to higher principles. The Transcendentalists urged their readers to become "whole" people, and this was possible only to the degree that the readers saw themselves as spiritual beings. The idea that humanity is synonymous with spirituality led to an important emphasis on practical ethics or what became the Transcendentalist "conduct of life." Many Transcendalists translated their concern with practical ethics into radical political action. Theodore Parker (1826–1862) and Henry David Thoreau were heavily involved in antislavery activities. Emerson gave lectures in support of abolitionism. Margaret Fuller wrote eloquently of women's rights. And Amos Bronson Alcott (1799–1888) was well known for his work in progressive school reform.

Transcendentalists deeply affected many of the ROMANTIC REFORM movements of the nineteenth century. The eloquent voices of reform came most notably from Ralph Waldo Emerson (1803–1882), Henry David Thoreau (1817–1862), and Margaret Fuller (1810–1850). Their ideas brought well-articulated arguments and reason to many reform causes—indeed, their legacies have influenced political protest and resistance movements throughout the twentieth century and even today.

Emerson and Social Reform

In his 1844 lecture "New England Reformers," Ralph Waldo Emerson observed that traditional New England churches were losing a fair number of their members to TEMPERANCE as well as to various movements of abolitionists and socialists. Emerson deduced that an impulse to wide-ranging social reform had taken hold of the New England mind. Although he was critical of those "partial" reformers who were only interested in one burning issue (such as prohibiting the use of alcohol), Emerson generally supported the spirit of reform. He was reluctant to lend his name to causes that were continually asking for his support, perhaps because he was wary of labels—which represented the kind of "group thinking" he despised and went against his belief in individualism. In the 1850s, however, Emerson relented and became a fervent advocate of abolitionism.

Emerson came to embrace social reform because he felt that the reform spirit promoted moral and intellectual vitality in social and political affairs. By questioning a certain custom or political belief, reformers made it difficult, if not impossible, for average citizens to continue lending their allegiance to the status quo in an unthinking or complacent fashion. Citizens would have to reflect on why exactly they held one belief and not another. Emerson wanted people to become self-conscious about the choices they made because it would make them more spiritual, self-reliant human beings—the ultimate aim of his Transcendental philosophy.

In "Man, the Reformer," Emerson writes that those involved in political and social reform believed in "an infinite worthiness in man." For humans to live up to their true spiritual potential, Emerson thought it was necessary to remove those things in society that impeded their progress. To seek freedom from the bonds of society was a part of human nature. Reform movements were concerned with specific social ills—slavery, alcoholism, ignorance. Emerson saw these acts of protest as representing the emancipation of all individuals from the lower levels of nature. For Emerson, humankind was struggling to live according to "higher laws."

Emerson believed passionately in the right to personal freedom of every person. It was this belief that led him to speak out against slavery and become one of the most famous supporters of the abolitionist movement. In speeches that resounded across the country, he spoke out about the Fugitive Slave Law, the Kansas-Nebraska Act, and the execution of John Brown. Emerson condemned the Fugitive Slave Law, which mandated the return of escaped slaves to their owners, calling it an immoral law and thus not binding to virtuous people: "An immoral

Fruitland Farms

The Alcott family founded a utopian Transcendentalist commune at the "Fruitlands" farmhouse near Harvard Village in Massachusetts.

law makes it a man's duty to break it, at every hazard. For virtue is the very self of every man. It is therefore a principle of law that an immoral contract is void, and that an immoral statute is void."

His eulogies for John Brown proved to be the most contentious of his antislavery speeches. Emerson gave two speeches about Brown, one at Boston on the occasion of Brown's execution and the other at Salem, Massachusetts, a few months later. In the first speech, Emerson declared Brown the "hero of Harper's Ferry," calling him a man of "courage and integrity," the "rarest of heroes, a pure idealist." In his second speech, Emerson praises Brown, but goes further to defend the abolitionists.

> Nothing is more absurd than to complain of this sympathy, or to complain of a party of men united in opposition to slavery. As well complain of gravity, or the ebb of the tide. Who makes the abolitionist? The slave-holder. The sentiment of mercy is the natural recoil which the laws of the universe provide to protect man-kind from destruction by savage passions.

Southern leaders were so incensed by Emerson's speeches that they resolved to disband the Union should the Republican candidate, Abraham Lincoln, be elected president.

The antislavery movement had become for Emerson inseparable from his philosophy. Emerson felt deeply the social responsibility of the individual to combat injustice. In the speech called "The Assault upon Mr. Sumner," Emerson concludes: "We must get rid of slavery or we must get rid of freedom."

Thoreau's *Civil Disobedience*

Perhaps the most famous text in the literature of romantic reform is Henry David Thoreau's essay, *Resistance to Civil Government* (1849), better known as *Civil Disobedience*. The occasion of the essay was Thoreau's refusal to pay a poll tax in the town of Concord in protest of the United States war with Mexico (1846–1848). Thoreau regarded the war as a conspiracy to seize Mexican lands and enable the expansion of southern slavery. Thoreau was jailed for his refusal to pay the tax. His essay is a defense of his actions as well as a treatise on the moral and political responsibilities of the citizen.

In *Civil Disobedience,* Thoreau argues that, in an ideal world, governments would be rendered unnecessary; citizens would have the requisite wisdom to rule themselves. Governments are simply

❧ MODERN CIVIL DISOBEDIENCE ❧

Thoreau's theory of civil disobedience influenced two important civil rights leaders in the twentieth century: Mohandas Karamchand Ghandi (1869–1948), who was deeply involved in the struggle against the might of the British Empire for India's national independence; and Dr. Martin Luther King, Jr. (1929–1968), who advocated nonviolent protest as a means of dismantling the legal system of racial segregation in the United States.

Gandhi was a proponent of passive resistance or satyagraha *(as it is known in the Gujarati language). He described satyagraha as "pure soul force"; the passive resister (or satyagrahi) wins out over the oppressor not by matching him blow for blow but by the power of love. By passively resisting the violence of the oppressor, the satyagrahi reveals to the oppressor that there is a greater power in this world than physical force: namely, the power of the human spirit to transcend a terrible situation. Ideally, oppressors begin to see their behaviors as less than human and realize that they cannot do evil to others without also degrading themselves.*

Martin Luther King, Jr., shared Ghandi's faith in the power of moral suasion. Moral suasion is the notion that a sinful individual can be reached in his or her heart—or conscience—and brought out of sin by persuasive moral argument. King tells us that Thoreau's essay convinced him "that non-cooperation with evil is as much a moral obligation as is cooperation with the good."

"expedient" or convenient as long as people remain at an un-Transcendental level. Certain low or technical issues (such as where to build a road) can be properly left to the government. But in the moral realm (on such matters as war and slavery), the individual must decide for him or herself on what course of action to follow. Thoreau counsels that we should be guided in our decisions by what is *right* rather than what is *legal*. The true measure of moral conduct is the "higher law" of God not the social law of humanity.

Thoreau suggests that we should be "men" rather than "subjects." In Thoreau's view, a man is an individual who acts for himself, whereas a subject is a slave to conformity. Thoreau says that a platoon of soldiers is a perfect example of men degraded into subjects. The soldier rejects the principle of self-reliance; he gives himself to the will of another to be used like a "machine." In the end, the soldier is not so much a "man" but a gun on legs, a small movable fort.

Thoreau believed that all citizens should act from principle and be prepared to struggle against the world for their beliefs. In a society where most people are mechanical subjects, the self-reliant citizen who acts in accordance with higher law is bound to run afoul of human law. In other words, the righteous individual will inevitably be viewed as a criminal. Hence it follows, that "the true place for a just man is in prison." A just man is much the superior of a mere voter because while the voter awaits to see if his vote will fall in with the majority, the just man who selflessly pursues the right is already in a "majority of one." Although he suffered imprisonment, Thoreau felt spiritually free because he acted in accordance with his own best nature by refusing to support what he considered an unjust war. In contrast, Thoreau's Concord neighbors, who did nothing to oppose the Mexican War, might be physically free to go about their business, but they were spiritually imprisoned in the jailhouse of social conformity. In short, they were mere "subjects" or moral slaves.

Thoreau says that the true reformer is a revolutionary, and the revolutionary is one who declares war against the state in his own fashion. By "war," Thoreau does not mean violent struggle. Like the Quakers, and others who disavow the use of violence as a political tool, Thoreau felt that the true force in the world, which transforms both individuals and institutions, is spiritual power. In the end, civil disobedience is a nonviolent form of protest, whose rightness and ultimate power comes from God.

Despite being opposed to violence, Thoreau found in John Brown a symbol of his Transcendental beliefs. In two powerful essays, "A Plea for Captain John Brown" (1859) and "The Last Days of John Brown" (1860), Thoreau presented Brown as romantic hero, the ultimate Transcendentalist who always strived to be equal to the high demands of the divine spirit. For Thoreau, Brown was a true patriot; because he loved his country, he hated to see it mired in the terrible sin of slavery. Brown was a radical revolutionary. He was radical because he struck at the roots of slavery, and he was a revolutionary not because he took up the gun but because of his willingness to sacrifice himself for a higher law. In short, he exemplifies what it means to "live deliberately," refusing to be merely a "subject." Thoreau goes on to explicitly link Brown to Jesus Christ. He intends the comparison as a way of saying that truly spiritual men will be crucified by the unenlightened as long as the world is based on inhumane relations. In the end, Thoreau believes it is the moral responsibility of

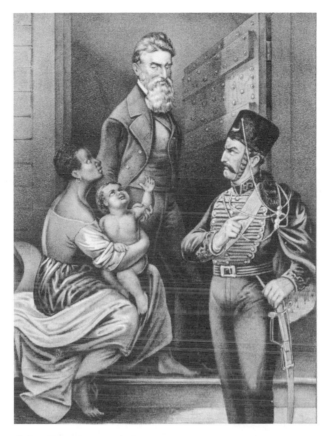

John Brown

The abolitionist John Brown (1800–1859) was convicted of treason for his attempt to foment a slave rebellion. Although hated by many, Brown was romanticized by poets and artists for his adamant opposition to slavery.

the individual to disrupt society when its government violates the higher laws of humankind's divine nature.

Margaret Fuller: Early American Feminist

The antislavery movement is the best example of romantic reformism in the nineteenth century. However, romantic reform was also central to the struggle for women's rights. Margaret Fuller was an important link between Transcendentalism and early American feminism. Fuller wrote in a letter (which was later published in her *Memoirs*) that she was not born to the "common womanly lot." She described herself as a "pilgrim" and a "sojourner" on the earth. She confessed that "very early I knew that the only object was to grow." Fuller accepted the Transcendentalist axiom that only people who were true to themselves—who understood the value of self-reliance—would experience personal growth.

Fuller was critical of "the common womanly lot" because it limited the growth of individual women to "wifedom" and "motherhood." In her book, *Woman in the Nineteenth Century* (1845), Fuller brings the Transcendentalist argument to bear on the question of women's rights. Fuller believes that men and women were the complements (or even the "compensations") of each other. As she put it, they were two halves of one thought. A woman could not develop without a man nor a man without a woman. According to Fuller, the era of "a truly human life" will only come about when men regard women as equal spiritual beings. Thus, the "lot" of woman was expressive of whether society was progressing. If one culture gave women more room for development than another, then it followed that the culture was farther along the road to social perfection. Just as the abolitionists used the existence of slavery to point to the prevalence of sin in the world, so feminist reformers used the oppression of women to highlight cultural inertia or backwardness.

Throughout the ages, says Fuller, men have treated women as inferior beings. Fuller argues that women ought to have every path open to them: The human soul can only aspire to perfection when its course is free. Two dominant stereotypes have been used to confine women: Mary the Madonna and Eve the temptress. Mary relates to the positive value of motherhood, whereas Eve bespeaks the negative value of feminine sexual wiles. Fuller suggests that nothing is so dreaded in women as "self-reliance" because it is a power that proves that women can attain individuality. Just as some romantics regarded children as intuitive beings, whereas others viewed Native Americans or peasants in a similar positive light, Fuller thought that

PROSLAVERY ANTIREFORMISTS

Many of the most severe critics of the Transcendentalists came from the South. In the proslavery manifesto called "Canniballs All! Or, Slaves Without Masters" (1857), Virginia lawyer George Fitzhugh advocated a return to a fundamentalist understanding of God, man, and country against the growing number of "isms" in the North:

> *But a "frequent recurrence to fundamental principles" is at war with the continued existence of all government, and is a doctrine fit to be sported only by the Isms of the North and the Red Republicans of Europe. With them no principles are considered established and sacred, nor will ever be. When, in time of revolution, society is partially disbanded, disintegrated and dissolved, the doctrine of Human Equality may have a hearing, and may be useful in stimulating rebellion; but it is practically impossible, and directly conflicts with all government, all separate property, and all social existence.*

Fitzhugh ridicules the social experiments of the North and argues that the romantic reformers did not understand human nature; they could not fathom "real" humanity, which was by nature brutal, selfish, and willing to do anything to survive—hence, we are cannibals all. It was because of man's brutal nature that government rightfully protected the rights of a white minority and ruled by force instead of consent. Christian morality was impractical, while slave society was a "natural morality." It was the idealism and liberalism of the northern intellectuals that was the real affront to humanity because it threatened to tear apart civilization. As opposed to achieving equality, the reformers wrongfully treaded upon the liberties of those who uphold God's natural order.

For Fitzhugh, all of the "isms" of the North led to a grave number of evils: "free love, free lands, free women and free churches." He enjoins conservatives of both the North and South to unite against the socialist reformers and fight to preserve the system of rule by privileged white men.

---

women had a "genius" for spiritual power. In her estimation, any woman who subjected herself to patriarchial stereotypes was not so much a woman as an "overgrown child." All women had it in them to discover the "secrets of nature."

Like Emerson, Fuller counseled reformers that they could not use base methods to achieve ideal goals; instead, "they must be severe lawgivers to themselves." Ultimately, Fuller felt that antislavery, feminism, and other reform movements were all addressing one and the same evil: the failure of human beings to achieve their proper nature as intelligent spirits. Fuller calls for "one creative energy, one incessant revelation," that would transcend all the divisions of race, class, and gender.

At this point, romantic reform passes into a general MILLENNIALISM, a powerful impulse in nineteenth-century America. A millennialist believes that the sinful world is drawing to an end, to be replaced by the thousand-year rule of Christ on earth. Many nineteenth-century Americans were drawn to millennialism because of their sense of impending catastrophe. Others thought that the millennium had already arrived to the degree that they believed that prosperity and justice for all were close at hand. It is evident that both Transcendentalism and the various utopian movements were part of this wider social culture of millennial dreams.

The tide of Romantic reform reaches its peak during the Civil War, after which the reformers found a less receptive audience for their ideas. Although slavery was abolished, there would be slow progress in human rights and social equality. It would take nearly another century, and the Civil Rights movements of the 1960s, before the country would see again popular support for social justice, political activism, and progressive idealism.

5. THE CRITICAL ROMANTICS

The Transcendentalists questioned everything—from religion to slavery—and proposed a new way of seeing man, God, and society. They conflicted often with formal traditions; indeed, they seemed intent on obliterating them. Equal and opposite reactions came, and with great vehemence, from all corners of society. Suddenly, despite being a young nation, opponents of social reform fought to preserve American traditions or institutions.

Southerners, for example, who once believed that slavery was an integral piece of a flawed economy, were now persuaded by writers such as George Fitzhugh (1806–1888) to defend slavery as part of southern heritage, "as a normal and natural institution," and as a "positive good, not a necessary evil." The Christian church, feeling besieged by the Transcendental pantheists and the growing number of new religions operating under the name of Christianity, splintered along the fault lines of liberal and conservative, progressive and fundamentalist.

Emerson Launches the Controversy

In many ways, Ralph Waldo Emerson (1803–1882) launched the controversy in one of the the most unlikely of places. It was at an address to the senior class of the Harvard Divinity school in July of 1838. He chose this particular event as a forum to expound upon some of his core Transcendental beliefs, and at the same time, to criticize what he believed were the failings of Christian practices and beliefs throughout the Harvard intellectual community. The speech that he gave was one of the most controversial speeches of the day. Many thought Emerson had gone too far. He had, among other things, asserted the humanity of Christ and argued for a God-like capability in all human beings. The speech caused waves of both approbation and revulsion. In either case, it led to a thorough review of core Christian values.

Harvard was scandalized. Emerson would not be invited back to his alma mater, despite being its most famous alumnus, until 1866, when the college granted him an honorary degree. A year and four days after Emerson's speech, the Association of the Alumni of the Cambridge Theological School invited Harvard professor and biblical scholar Andrews Norton to refute Emerson's speech. The title of Norton's speech was the "Latest Form of Infidelity," and he took the occasion, though never naming Emerson directly, to attack Emerson's theology. In the speech, Norton criticizes the new religions for importing European ideas to America. "We have indeed but little to guard us," states Norton, "against the influence of the depraving literature and noxious speculations which flow in among us from Europe." His talk was largely theological, centering on the belief in miracles, which Emerson had likened to superstition. Norton contends that miracles are essential to Christianity because they reveal the awesome power of God. For Norton, the Transcendentalist did not fear this "appalling God" nearly enough. Transcendentalists believed so much in the power of the individual that they, in their vanity, lacked proper faith and falsely tried to understand God through human reason.

Emerson's speech at Harvard rekindled the ongoing debate between liberal and conservative theologies, namely Unitarianism versus Calvinism. Northern conservatives such as Norton sought to reaffirm traditional beliefs of Christianity that the new religions were leaving behind. FUNDAMENTALISM took hold in the South, largely as a backlash against the social reformers of the North, as the antislavery movement became synonymous with liberal theology. A NEO-CALVINISM began to be formulated not just in the South but among the growing number of Christian conservatives. A renewed emphasis on ORIGINAL SIN and "Grace"–the belief that God chooses who will be saved–became widely used counterarguments to Transcendentalism.

What began as a theological debate escalated dramatically. Controversy followed both Emerson and the Transcendentalists, who had pursued their ideology from religious circles to the wider social and political theaters. In his defenses of abolitionism and John Brown, Emerson repeatedly assailed the character of southern leaders. The political and economic forces behind the "institution of slavery" chose to attack Transcendentalists as well as antislavery advocates. In terms of political, religious, and philosophical outlook, the opposition was largely conservative and reactionary. In time, it became a full-blown counter movement against romantic social reform.

Prominent southern politicians, notably John C. Calhoun, advanced this counterview. A one-time vice president of the United States, senator, and representative from South Carolina, Calhoun was one of the most vociferous defenders of slavery. In his "Disquisition on Government" (1840), he writes:

> It follows, from what has been stated, that it is a great and
> dangerous error to suppose that all people are equally
> entitled to liberty. It is a reward to be earned, not a blessing

🕭 CULTURAL CRITICS 🕭

The critical romantics felt ambivalence about the progress of American society. On the one hand, they viewed the United States as a stage to explore new possibilities in human culture; on the other hand, they thought that too many Americans were foolishly willing to identify the pursuit of happiness with the pursuit of riches. Poe, for example, was deeply critical of the elevation of "commodity" over culture. Poe blamed the decline of cultural taste on what he called the "aristocracy of dollars." Poe believed that the development of American literature was seriously hindered by the poor cultural standards among American readers, which prevented them from properly appreciating works of genius.

The other problem facing the serious American author, as Hawthorne saw it, was the lack of appropriate materials for a truly American romance. In the preface to The Marble Faun *(1859, 1860), Hawthorne observed that whereas Italy was rich in the architectural ruins and cultural traditions that were the proper objects of the romancer, the United States was singularly lacking in these things:*

No author, without a trial, can conceive of the difficulty of writing a romance about a country where there is no shadow, no antiquity, no mystery, no picturesque and gloomy wrong, nor anything but a commonplace prosperity, in broad and simple daylight, as is happily the case with my dear native land.

---

to be gratuitously lavished on all alike—a reward reserved for the intelligent, the patriotic, the virtuous and deserving—and not a boon to be bestowed on a people too ignorant, degraded and vicious, to be capable either of appreciating or of enjoying it.

Calhoun rejects the notion of the Transcendentalists' belief in equality; rather, he suggests that liberty be limited to the deserving, lest the greater commonwealth fall prey to the lower ranks of humanity.

From New England theologians to southern politicians, the threads behind these diverse critics of Transcendentalism are rejections of its idealism. Transcendentalists were committed to social PERFECTIONISM: they felt that various social reforms were pathways for bringing spirit into the world. Behind this feeling was an optimism about the ultimate relationship between human beings and a merciful, loving God. Many of their critics did not share this optimism. The Transcendentalists, they argued, failed to see both the violence in nature and the evil that humankind repeatedly demonstrated throughout its history. Any understanding of theology or government had to take into account this "real" view of humanity.

Poe, Hawthorne, and Melville

The Transcendentalists believed in the inherent goodness within nature. Nature was a harmonious unity. Emerson even went so far as to deny the existence of evil, which he defined as nothing more than the absence of good. For Emerson, good only had to appear and evil dissipated, as light overcomes darkness. Every human being possessed this inner knowledge of the good and an equal capacity for goodness. However, there were romantic writers who strongly disagreed with the Transcendentalist position. Edgar Allan Poe (1809–1849), Nathaniel Hawthorne (1804–1864), and Herman Melville (1819–1891) were all critical of the metaphysics of nature that Transcendentalism rested upon.

Poe, Hawthorne, and Melville were suspicious of the idea that the world was a harmonious unity. They emphasized in their writings the ambiguous, discordant, and chaotic aspects of human experience. They were not disposed to deny the reality of evil. Emerson's rejection of evil seemed to these writers an evasion of real moral questions. If one assumes that evil is an absolute reality—that some things are wholly bad and do not lead to anything good—then it follows that the Transcendentalist's belief in a benevolent nature must be wrong.

Poe, Hawthorne, and Melville accepted the Calvinist doctrine of original human sin—the human propensity for evil. Consequently, they were deeply suspicious of the perfectionist schemes of utopian reformers and Transcendentalists. Perfectionism supposed the impossible: that the temptation to sin might eventually disappear. Poe, Hawthorne, and Melville were concerned to show that a significant part of human nature (much more than the Transcendentalists were ready to admit) was on the side of the devil. Human beings were not simply oriented towards truth, beauty, and justice; the human heart also beat to the rhythms of illusion, cruelty, and power. If the Transcendentalists were moved by the general notions of revelation and redemption—that one might come to the light of God out of the darkness of sin—then the critical romantics were inspired by the neo-Calvinist ideas of divine mystery and damnation.

Hawthorne's Fallen Humanity

In the winter of 1840, Nathaniel Hawthorne (1804–1864) became one of the original investors in the utopian community of Brook Farm. In the spring of 1841, Hawthorne went to live in the community, along with its founding members George and Sophia Ripley and others. Brook Farm was a haven for Transcendentalists. The farm was visited regularly by the likes of Margaret Fuller, William Henry Channing, and Emerson. However, within the year, Hawthorne withdrew from the commune. He had become dissatisfied with the experience and disillusioned with certain members of the community. Out of his disenchantment with the experience grew a deepening intellectual skepticism regarding Transcendentalism, specifically as it related to the perfectibility of human beings and the nature of evil in the world.

Although the experiment may have failed, it led to a theme that would pervade Hawthorne's later works: the fallibility of human beings. "The progress of the world," Hawthorne writes, "at every step, leaves some evil or wrong on the path behind it, which the unrest of mankind, or their own set purpose, could never have found the way to rectify." Clearly, Hawthorne had set his mind against utopias and the optimism of social reform as embodied by the Transcendentalists.

In 1846, Hawthorne published the short story collection *Mosses from an Old Manse*. In one story, "The New Adam and Eve," Hawthorne imagines the return of Adam and Eve after a complete obliteration of the human race. In tongue-and-cheek fashion, he describes Adam and Eve trying to make sense out of human civilization. Their view of the world is romantic; they are continually drawn to nature, to the sky especially, and are alienated by the cold confines of the city. Hawthorne's distaste for humankind can be seen in the climax, where Adam almost falls prey to knowledge in a library, which held "all the wrong principles and worse practice, the pernicious examples and mistaken rules of life." By suggesting that books would tempt Adam into a second fall, Hawthorne presents a dark view of human knowledge. The "disastrous lore" of learning and theories, perhaps such as those found in Transcendentalism, are symbols of humankind's loss of its Edenic nature. Books, the trees of knowledge, only reflect humankind's fall from grace.

In 1850, Hawthorne would publish his masterpiece *The Scarlet Letter*. In this work especially, Hawthorne dramatizes his philosophy of good and evil. For Hawthorne, good and evil are inseparable. They are part and parcel of the human drama in which divine goodness spars continually with demonic evil.

❧ STARVING ARTISTS ❧

Hawthorne, Melville, and Poe all struggled with the profession of writing. All three had families to support and wished they could make a better living through their art. True literary artists had to struggle for readership, while the publishing industry exploited untalented writers. In an 1855 letter to his publisher, Hawthorne complained about the literary market being cornered by a "damned mob of scribbling women." Poe never achieved a comfortable sense of authorship. He was forced to get by as a HACK JOURNALIST—someone who just writes for money, not for art's sake—even as he remained committed to serious literature. He turned to story writing because he thought that fiction was more marketable than poetry.

For his part, Melville acquired fame for his novels Typee *(1846) and* Omoo *(1847) and decent earnings, but he never really approached the success of those two novels again. Melville never felt free to write what he wanted. In a letter to Hawthorne, Melville wrote: "What I feel most moved to write, that is banned,—it will not pay. Yet, altogether, write the other way I cannot. So the product is a final hash, and all my books are botches." Poor sales of Melville's last books demoralized him greatly, and he ultimately retired from the writing profession decades before his death.*

We see this war between good and evil in Rev. Dimmesdale, whose sins of adultery and deceit eat away at him:

> To the untrue man, the whole universe is false—it is impalpable—it shrinks to nothing within his grasp. And he himself, in so far as he shows himself in a false light, becomes a shadow, or, indeed, ceases to exist. The only truth, that continued to give Mr. Dimmesdale a real existence on this earth, was the anguish in his inmost soul, and the undissembled expression of it in his aspect. Had he once found power to smile, and wear a face of gayety, there would have been no such man!

Hawthorne paints a brilliant psychological portrait of Dimmesdale's tortured soul, caught at the nexus of good and evil. The shadows of his conscience are, for Hawthorne, a metaphor for all human conscience, which must always be a place of conflict between our better and baser selves.

It is in the character of Roger Chillingworth, however, that Hawthorne poses his most telling indictment of the nature of evil in humankind. Hawthorne asks us to ponder what moral end is served by Roger Chillingworth's cruel treatment of the disgraced clergyman, Arthur Dimmesdale. The answer leads his readers to a dark conception of the hold evil may have over some. These people, he suggests, are beyond redemption.

In 1852, Hawthorne returned to the experiment at Brook Farm in his satirical tragedy *The Blithedale Romance.* The novel is filled with Hawthorne's wry comments about the folly of utopian thought. Theories and philosophies may be all well and good, but human beings will always be in conflict, both with the theory and among themselves. In the end, Hawthorne presents stinging indictments of the social idealists he once communed with at Brook Farm.

The Blithedale tragedy acts as a parable of how the best intentions can fall prey to the worst motivations. Evil triumphs over good. The novel's devil is the character Westervelt. "His black eyes sparkled at me," says the narrator, Miles Coverdale, "whether with fun or malice I knew not, but certainly as if the Devil were peeping out of them." Clearly, Hawthorne means to recollect the serpent in the Garden. The Eden allusion provides the moral point of the tragedy. Humanity had its chance in Eden. In their fallen state, human beings may want to recreate that Eden—just as the social reforms tried to create utopias and fought for social justice and equality—but paradise is forever beyond humankind's reach. While one may intuit the beauty of God's grace and the beauty of nature, one will always fall prey to the temptations of sin. There is, in the end, no possibility of heaven on earth.

Melville's Mysterious Nature

As one who had been at sea on a whaling ship, Melville was well aware of the violent, bloody side of nature. He was prepared to consider the possibility that nature might have been created for a purpose that we cannot discern. For Melville, the wisdom of God surpassed human understanding. In his novel *Pierre; or the Ambiguities* (1852), Melville writes:

> Say what some poets will, Nature is not so much her own
> ever-sweet interpreter, as the mere supplier of that cunning

🖎 DEATH AND NINETEENTH-CENTURY ROMANTICS 🖎

A fact of life in the nineteenth century was the firsthand knowledge of the fragility of human life. In nearly all of the biographies of the great romantics, one will find tragedy. Edgar Allan Poe was orphaned at the age of three after his father abandoned the family and his mother died. Herman Melville was 13 when his father died. Family financial problems forced him to take work on ships as a young adult. Emerson's life was filled with tragedy. His father died when he was eight. All three of his brothers died, his first wife at 20, and his older son at five. Henry David Thoreau's brother John died of lockjaw, after cutting himself shaving. Thoreau went to Walden Pond, in part, to write a memorial to his brother. Margaret Fuller's father died in 1835, which brought financial problems for the family. The eldest, she became responsible for the education of her younger siblings and was the main breadwinner of the family.

Between 1813 and 1819, all four of James Fenimore Cooper's brothers died, as did his mother. Two of his children also died, both just under two years of age. Cooper, like so many of the other romantics, turned to writing, partly as a response to the tragedy. While dealing with death was a fact of life for nineteenth-century Americans—high infant mortality rates put average life expectancy roughly around 44 years—the death of close family members clearly had an impact on the philosophy and writings of the romantics.

---

alphabet, whereby selecting and combining as he pleases, each man reads his own peculiar lesson according to his own peculiar mind and mood.

Emerson supposes that nature has one message for all: the primacy of spirit. In contrast, Melville suggests that human beings decipher what meaning they want, according to their own psychology. Human understanding often has nothing to do with outside reality, but rather colors the world according to individual perception.

Like Hawthorne, Melville saw human beings as not always involved in the quest for the light and good in nature. People were as much concerned with transgression, or going beyond boundaries, as they were with searching for truth. Captain Ahab in Melville's *Moby Dick* is modeled on mythological figures such as Faust, Prometheus,

Whaling ship
This illustration vividly portrays the nature of Ahab's quest in Melville's *Moby Dick*. The image of tiny men silhouetted against the body of the immense beast emphasizes the enormity of the challenge Ahab has set himself.

Icarus, and Satan. Faust sold his soul to the devil for power and knowledge; Prometheus dared to steal fire from the gods and was cruelly punished; Icarus aspired to fly and plummeted to earth when his waxen wings melted under the sun; and Satan, a fallen angel, was cast out of heaven for defying the will of God. These figures are all overreachers—they all aim at something that is sinful or illicit. They all suffer the penalty of damnation or some other species of terrible punishment. It is in this class of overreachers that Ahab falls. Ahab is heroic to the degree that he refuses all limits on human aspiration, but at the same time, his HUBRIS makes him morally dangerous.

Nature, for its part, always exists outside human perception, always mysterious and ultimately unknowable. The sea is symbolic of this mysterious nature: "one knows not what sweet mystery about this sea, whose gently awful stirrings seem to speak of some hidden soul beneath." However, the greatest symbol of this mysterious nature is Moby Dick. Unlike Emerson's view of nature, which is both knowable and transcendent, the white whale symbolically eludes its pursuers. Nature is thus unattainable.

Melville is most fascinated by humankind's perception of nature—this, he asserts, can be known. Ahab's tortured soul transforms nature into evil:

> All evil, to crazy Ahab . . . [was] visibly personified, and made practically assailable in Moby Dick. He piled upon the whale's white hump the sum of all the general rage and hate felt by his whole race from Adam down.

The whale, of course, is no more good than evil. It has an objective reality outside of human understanding. The reason for the inability of humankind to grasp nature lies in the allusion to "the race of Adam down." Perhaps the most Calvinistic of all the romantic critics, Melville believed that the fall of Adam and Eve prevented humankind from ever discerning the truth of God's mysteries.

Melville's last published novel *Confidence Man* (1857) pursues humankind's fallen nature down darker avenues, increasingly calling into question the usefulness of language for arriving at the truth, and worse, humankind's propensity for inventing lies and falling for them. For Melville, human beings were always flawed and fallen. People's natures prevented them from ever apprehending divine truth. His growing skepticism may have led to his eventual abandonment of fiction. At any case, he did not publish any more novels for over three decades before his death in 1891.

Poe and the Art of Death

In Poe's writing, the great fact of death—whether by disease, violence, or accident—symbolically hints at the difficulty of truly comprehending the purpose of life. Poe questions the Transcendentalist's belief in the ability to comprehend the world of the spirit while living. For Poe, death was the only point of entry into the infinite world of spirit, which was beyond understanding. His art often enjoins the reader to contemplate his or her own death in order to appreciate the terrible beauty of human mortality.

In his essay "The Philosophy of Composition," Poe observed that the death of a beautiful woman was "the most poetical topic in the world." He sees this death as symbol of the mutability or instability of human ideals. In dying, the beautiful woman, as perceived by her beloved, passes from matter to spirit, from desire to memory, and from actuality to imagination. The beauty of the beautiful dead woman becomes infinite because it is no longer attached to its finite body. Thus, beauty is understood as spirit. Unfortunately, as spirit, the woman herself is now wholly beyond the reach of her admirer. Many of Poe's poems such as "To Helen" and "Annabel Lee," and some of his stories, "Liegia" and "The Oval Portrait," consider this theme.

Poe was drawn to the elements of GOTHIC ROMANCE. The gothic emphasized terror as a fundamental emotion. Poe used this GENRE to explore dramatic ways of causing his readers to confront death. Poe's stories typically involve death and depravity, madness, cruelty, and perversity. Characters are often diseased—their minds collapse, their bodies rot. Poe seemed to believe that the romantic way to beauty was inseparable from every species of human ugliness. In Poe's story, "The Black Cat," the narrator speaks of coming under the influence of the "spirit of perverseness," which makes him do evil things precisely because he knows they are evil and ought not to be done. Poe calls perverseness "one of the primary impulses of the human heart."

Poe wrote the prose-poem, *Eureka*, shortly before his death. *Eureka* is about the origin and purpose of the universe. Using an intuitive form of reasoning that he calls "soul reveries," Poe argues that all the atoms of the material universe derive from the original unity of God, but since the act of creation the atoms have been caught in a cosmic tension between the tendency to reunite and the tendency to remain apart. Should the atoms recover their unity, all matter would

❧ THE UNHAPPY LIFE OF EDGAR ALLAN POE ❧

On October 3, 1849, as he walked down a city street, Mr. J.W. Walker of Baltimore happened upon a semi-conscious person lying in the gutter. He arranged for this person to be taken to Washington College Hospital. The man awoke the following day in acute despair. He soon fell into delirium, and on the afternoon of October 7, 1849, he died. The man in question was named Edgar Allan Poe. It is not known if Poe suffered an epileptic fit or a mental collapse, alcohol poisoning, or perhaps even, according to a current theory, rabies. In many respects his mysterious death was of a piece with his unhappy life.

Edgar Allan Poe was born in Boston, Massachusetts, in January 1809. After his father abandoned his family and his mother died of tuberculosis in 1811, the infant orphan Edgar was reared (but was never formally adopted) by John and Frances Allan of Richmond, Virginia. Although John Allan wanted him to enter the business world, Poe went to the University of Virginia in 1826, where he behaved badly, drinking heavily and gambling himself into considerable debt. Forced to give up his studies, he enlisted in the military, and in 1830 was admitted to West Point. There, Poe continued in his bad ways; in 1831 he was court-martialed and dishonorably dismissed.

In 1836, he married his 13-year-old cousin, Virginia Clemm. He held several jobs in publishing, but all came to an end because he was disagreeable and contentious. In 1847, Poe was left in despair by the death of his wife. In October 1849, on his way back North after a trip to Richmond, Poe stopped at Baltimore, where Mr. J.W. Walker was to find him half out of his mind, lying in the gutter.

---

cease to exist, as the finite would once again become the infinite (i.e., God). In this way, the universe is a rational design of God. However, that design prevents the finite world from joining the infinite in any way other than through the imagination—or death.

In the end, Poe felt death was to be faced with both awe and horror, because it is and always will be unknown. However, his romantic sensibility, that element in Poe that finds beauty in death, and wonder in the cosmos, suggests a higher purpose. This combination of both fear and awe, are, for Poe, the proper emotions for humankind when contemplating God.

Edgar Allan Poe

Edgar Allan Poe (1809–1849) was known for masterful poetry and short stories that explored the darker aspects of the human imagination. In this daguerrotype, according to one of his friends, Sarah Whitman, he looks like someone "immediately after being snatched back from the ultimate world's end of horror."

In all of the critical romantics, we find the same tendency to see the "imperfect" sides of the human condition, and as such they are the artistic counterbalance to the Transcendentalists' cheery optimism. Their darker views of human nature set the stage for the later movements toward realism in American art.

6. ROMANTICISM AND POETIC VOICE

While America had claimed political freedom from the Old World, culturally it still struggled mightily for independence from its European predecessors. Cultural critics throughout the nineteenth century complained that its writers were still too heavily influenced by European models. In "American Literature; Its Position in the Present Time, and Prospects for the Future" (1846), Margaret Fuller writes: "Books which imitate or represent the thoughts and life of Europe do not constitute an American literature." Fuller laments that the nation had not yet found its poetic voice, and would not do so, until writers, publishers, and readers banded together to create a climate that would yield a great American literature.

The Call for a National Literature

In his *Remarks on National Literature* (1830), the influential Unitarian minister William Ellery Channing (1780–1842) argues the importance of literature in shaping the American character. He observes that literature is among "the most powerful methods of exalting the character of a nation, of forming a better race of men." The literary work advances moral and cultural ideals, and to this extent it also points out the flaws in the real world.

For Channing, an American literature held the potential to reveal the real nature of humanity, because, for the first time in history, the imaginative writer was able to consider human experience in the terms of a fully democratic society. Unlike European literature, with its deep grounding in feudalism and aristocracies, an American literature would arise out of higher moral principles and universal truths upon which the country was founded. With so much at stake, Channing implores his audience to rise to the occasion. He calls for a national American literature. He suggests that American writers forget about the Old World and concentrate on capturing the American experience in new and artistic ways.

Channing's arguments influenced the most famous call for a national literature, Ralph Waldo Emerson's "The American Scholar" (1837). Like Channing, Emerson writes that Americans "have listened too long to the courtly muses of Europe." For Emerson, it is crucial for every generation to have a literature that is "active," reflecting its own place and time in history: "Each age, it is found, must write its own books; or rather, each generation for the next succeeding." By revering the old traditions, American critics, scholars, and writers fail to seize upon their cultural moment. Emerson's hope is "that poetry will revive and lead in a new age" in American thought.

Emerson believes that the poet is a crucial figure in any age. In his essay "The Poet," Emerson calls the poet "representative"—he stands out among the crowd as a whole person. The poet is "complete" because he is not imprisoned within the world of "sensuous fact." According to Emerson, a poet is not defined by his technical skill with words; only the one who knows and tells the truth about spirit merits the title "poet." The true poet, says Emerson, is a "liberating god," because he breaks up established beliefs, and, in so doing, keeps thought active, always in pursuit of truth.

Emerson declared that "America is a poem in our eyes," but American writers could not yet see it. He writes:

> Our log-rolling, our stumps and their politics, our fisheries, our Negroes and Indians, our boats and our repudiations, the wrath of rogues and the pusillanimity of honest men, the northern trade, the southern planting, the western clearing, Oregon and Texas, are yet unsung.

ELIZABETH PEABODY: TRANSCENDENTAL ACTIVIST

Elizabeth Palmer Peabody (1804–1894) was the sister-in-law of Nathaniel Hawthorne (1804–1864) and Horace Mann (1796–1859) and was well connected with all the major figures of Transcendentalism. As a young girl, she was raised on the sermons of William Ellery Channing. She led a remarkably diverse life with many different careers. She ran the West Street Bookstore in Boston, providing the Transcendentalists with a gathering place. She also had a career as a publisher of the famous Transcendentalist journal The Dial, *as well as works by Channing, Hawthorne, and Thoreau.*

Her greatest contribution was in the area of education. She ran a number of schools, and later in life, she and her sister Mary worked to establish kindergartens in schools across America. A Transcendental activist her entire life, she moved from cause to cause, trying to improve society through knowledge and good works.

The American poet who would capture the remarkable complexities of southern slavery, the western frontier, folk culture, politics, must be dynamic, able to synthesize so many different parts into a coherent whole. The one who could do such a thing would help America at last discover its own national literature.

Like so many of his contemporary critics, Emerson concludes that no such poet exists anywhere on the American scene. However,

thc original poetic voices of America that Emerson and the Transcendentalists were seeking, the great works of American literature, would
soon be heard in the poetry of a diverse group of Americans: a Harvard professor, a common working man, and a reclusive woman.

Longfellow and the Mythic Past

Henry Wadsworth Longfellow (1807–1882) was the most famous
American poet of his era. His easy rhythms and narrative skill brought
him international fame. However, when Margaret Fuller writes of
those who "write among us in the methods and of the thoughts of
Europe" as being "colonists and useful schoolmasters to our people
in a transition," Longfellow's early works come to mind. In short
poems such as "Endymion" (1842), we see in Longfellow the European style: classical themes encased in perfect IAMBIC METER, regular
rhyme schemes, and poetic language. The poems are skillful, yet im-
personal, and formulaic. A poet well-schooled in the European arts—
he was fluent in eight languages—Longfellow was known for verse
that tenderly mixed sentimental messages with simple, clear imagery.
It was Longfellow, for example, in his poem "A Psalm of Life" (1839)
who penned the famous lines:

> Lives of great men all remind us
> We can make our lives sublime,
> And, departing, leave behind us
> Footprints on the sands of time.

In 1855, the former Harvard professor took a dramatic step for-
ward in both his style and subject when he published *The Song of
Hiawatha*. He conceived the poem as an EPIC romance of the American Indians, the first Americans, whose hold on the land was fast dis-
appearing. Like James Fenimore Cooper (1789–1851), Longfellow
felt that the national character of the United States was partly defined by what it had absorbed from America's first inhabitants. He im-
plored his readers in the prologue to the poem:

> Listen to these wild traditions,
> To this Song of Hiawatha!
> Ye who love a nation's legends,
> Love the ballads of a people.

In the poem, Longfellow brings to life the myths and traditions of
Native Americans, setting them in a meter and style conducive to
English narrative poetry. Its regular beats and use of exotic Native

American names and words were innovative and imaginative. His romantic vision struck a chord with a wide audience hungry for art about America's original inhabitants and fueled further interest in Native American culture.

The poem was also extremely successful because of Longfellow's growing gifts as a poetic storyteller. By taking on American subjects, he began to stake claim as the national poet of his age. His poem "The Courtship of Miles Standish" (1858) creates a fictional romance of the PILGRIMS. In poems such as "Paul Revere's Ride" (1860), Longfellow masterfully combines storytelling and lyric poetry to create a national myth. The poem begins with the famous lines

> Listen, my children, and you shall hear
> Of the midnight ride of Paul Revere,
> On the eighteenth of April, in Seventy-five;
> Hardly a man is now alive
> Who remembers that famous day and year.

Longfellow narrates the tale as if it is a bedtime story for children. Its simplicity is misleading, however. His poem immortalizes Paul Revere's feats, turning the legend into national myth. By framing the poem as a children's story, he suggests that it is a story worth passing down from one generation to the next.

Longfellow has been passed over by contemporary literary critics largely because his style has an old-fashioned quality, and his use of traditional narrative poetry is no longer in vogue. Nevertheless, his historical popularity—if not his talents as narrative poet—place Longfellow among the ranks of original American poets. One suspects he will be reclaimed by future generations of Americans.

Whitman and the Poetry of America

The Song of Hiawatha is a romance of an American mythic past. However, in 1855, the same year in which Longfellow published his epic, a book of five poems appeared whose central topic was the romance of the American future. The book was entitled *Leaves of Grass*. It had no name on the front page, but the author was pictured, standing casually but proudly, in the dress of a common working man, his shirt collar open, his hat at an angle. We learn nearly half-way through the first poem, the epic "Song of Myself," that the author's name is Walt Whitman, "an American, one of the roughs, a KOSMOS." *Leaves of Grass* was designed, set to type, and printed by Whitman himself. He sent copies to the literary journals. Reviews of the book were mostly unfavorable, as critics condemned Whitman's ineptitude as a poet, and his penchant for obscene and vulgar themes.

Whitman was not easily deterred. He had immense confidence in his own abilities. After reading Emerson, he became certain that he himself was "The Poet" Emerson described in his essays. Whitman said that he was "simmering, simmering, simmering," and that the experience of reading Emerson brought him to the boil. He was audacious enough to send a copy of Leaves of Grass to Emerson. Whitman could only have been delighted by Emerson's reply. Emerson complimented Whitman on his "free and brave thought," the same phrase Emerson used to describe the independent thinker in "The American Scholar." Emerson praised Leaves of Grass as authentic American literature. With remarkable foresight, he said to Whitman: "I greet you at the beginning of a great career."

In his preface to the first edition of Leaves of Grass, Whitman makes plain his ambition to become THE American national poet. Whitman claims that he is indeed the embodiment of Emerson's great poet, and that his greatness re-

❧ THE CAREERS OF ❧ WALT WHITMAN

Although he was not formally educated, Whitman worked as a journalist and printer for many years; he also tried his hand at school teaching and carpentry. At the height of his journalism days, in the 1840s and 1850s, Whitman edited the Brooklyn Daily Freeman. The paper was closely linked to the Free Soil Party, whose motto was, "Free Soil, free labor, free men."

During the CIVIL WAR, Whitman served the Union as an army nurse working in a field hospital in Washington, D.C. There he witnessed firsthand the horrors of war. His journal is filled with GROTESQUE descriptions of rotting dead bodies and amputated limbs. Whitman took the role of nurse seriously: He attended to the physical needs of the soldiers and also provided moral support, writing letters, bringing fruit, and reading to them. His experiences there resulted in the book of poetry Drum Taps (1865).

sides in his perfect understanding of the spirit of American reality. In league with Emerson, he describes the United States as "essentially the greatest poem." Whitman seizes upon America as the theme of his poetic vision. His poetry is a romantic celebration of democracy and the common people. The key to Whitman's romanticism lies in his wish to spiritualize democracy, to make democracy, as it were, the new religion.

Whitman captures the newness of the American experience by rejecting the old models of poetry. The traditional epic deals with exceptional people, in a high poetic style. Epics begin with a somber invocation to the divine spirits: Homer begins the Iliad and Odyssey with invocations to the Muse; Milton invokes the heavenly spirit in his opening lines of *Paradise Lost*. Whitman alludes to this epic invocation at the opening lines of *Leaves of Grass* with the simple "I celebrate myself." In so doing, Whitman rejects the traditional epic to assert his own individuality and the independence of his poetry.

The break with tradition is clear in the form, tone, and style Whitman employs. Whitman writes in FREE VERSE—there is little rhyming, the meter is irregular, and the language of the poem sounds like the cadences of everyday speech. In other words, Whitman writes in a form that matches his subject. He writes of ordinary Americans in an "unpoetic" voice that is both conversational and approachable.

Whitman's poetry resists simple description, but one can pick out some characteristic Whitmanesque themes, of which three are central: the city, unity in diversity, and the individual.

The City

Romantics were skeptical about the spiritual value of urban life. If Nature were a temple where one might commune with God, then the city, which covered over the natural landscape, could well be regarded as an impediment to spirit. As Emerson put it in "The Poet," if you fill your head with Boston and New York, you will be blind to the "wisdom" of pine forests.

Whitman, however, was a different sort of romantic. He saw the city as a kind of nature, *human* nature. Cities, especially Manhattan, had a great spirit of their own. In many of Whitman's poems, we accompany the poetic "I" as it loiters and loafs about the streets, taking note of the fantastic range of urban activities, work, play, and crime, vice of all sorts, shopping, driving or merely walking. In his great poem, "Crossing Brooklyn Ferry," Whitman writes: "I loved well those cities, loved well the stately and rapid river, / The Men and women I saw were all near to me." For Whitman, the city contained great spiritual value because it brought individuals together, made them act as one, and ultimately advanced the spirit of democracy.

Unity in Diversity

Whitman was drawn to the image of leaves of grass because when one looks at a field it seems one expanse of green, but on closer inspection it reveals itself to be millions of individual blades, each perfectly separate and unique. For Whitman, democracy is the true political philosophy of the spirit, because it properly recognizes that liberty, equality and fraternity are the only real measures of what it is to be human. Whitman thought that the nineteenth century was an age of progressive democracy and that it was bound, therefore, to be

Walt Whitman
An iconic symbol of the American poet, Walt Whitman (1819–1892) was one of the most photographed authors of the nineteenth century.

the era of the *ensemble* or what he called the *en masse* (a French phrase meaning "as a whole").

An ENSEMBLE is a group of musicians working together. Where Emerson and Thoreau were suspicious of the crowd as a spiritual threat to the integrity of the individual, Whitman suggests that the crowd or mass is made up of individuals, all actively contributing to the art of democracy, that is, the making of a free and equal society. In poems like "Faces," and "City of Orgies," Whitman celebrates the urban crowd as a sort of prophecy of the future perfect society, where all human beings will become one, even as they remain individuals.

Individuality

In "Song of Myself," the poet assures us that we must make our own journeys through the world, that no one can do our traveling for us. Although he affirmed that the principle of the average person was a worthy and necessary aspect of democratic culture, Whitman, like Emerson, also extolled the virtue of the extraordinary person. In his 1882 essay *Democratic Vistas,* Whitman argued that modern mass society, with its crowds, groups, and classes, its faceless bureaucracies and machine-like armies, required the compensating principle of what he termed a "rich, luxuriant, varied PERSONALISM." By "personalism" he meant that the self is the fundamental reality; things are real only to the degree that they are experienced by actual persons.

Whitman felt that the essence of personalism was contained in the spiritual fact that all people are individuals. To treat people as *individuals* is necessarily to treat them as *persons*. Whitman agreed with Emerson and Thoreau, that the individual should value his or her own personhood above all else.

The Body Electric

Throughout his career, Whitman declared himself the poet of the body as well as the soul. He did not regard one as being higher than the other; he saw them as the complements of each other. The body without the spirit was mere animal flesh, but the soul without the body was a thing so abstract that it could not be said to exist. The clearest statement of Whitman's views on the relationship between the soul and the body is contained in the poem, "I Sing the Body Electric." The poet reflects:

A man's body at auction
(For before the war I often go to the slave-mart and watch the sale,)

I help the auctioneer, the sloven
does not know half his business.
Gentlemen look on this wonder,
Whatever the bids of the bidders they cannot be high enough
for it.

Whitman uses the slave auction to make a point about the wonderful divinity of the human body. When people are enslaved, they are treated as mere bodies, as though they lack a human spirit. Whitman states that the auctioneer and the bidders falsely attempt to put a price on the slave's body because they are wholly blind to his soul. For Whitman, the soul and the body are inseparable. Nearly every function of the body is inherently spiritual. For this reason Whitman celebrated sexuality and eating, athletics and loafing, as worthy spiritual pursuits. Whitman opposed the Puritan emphasis on natural depravity—he thought that human beings were most unnatural when they suppressed, or felt guilty about, the pleasures of the body. The body was "electric," because it was wholly infused with the primordial energy of nature itself.

Emily Dickinson and the Nation Within

While both Longfellow and Whitman enjoyed the celebrity of their status as great American poets, Emily Dickinson (1830–1860) remained anonymous her entire life. In a poem that begins "I'm Nobody," Dickinson writes,

I'm Nobody! Who are you?
Are you—Nobody—Too?
Then there's a pair of us!
Don't tell! they'd advertise—you know!

How dreary—to be—Somebody!
How public—like a Frog –
To tell one's name—the livelong June—
To an admiring Bog!

In this whimsical, defiant, and self-reliant poem, Dickinson proudly proclaims her anonymity. Unwilling to promote herself, she would pass her life out of the public eye. She had friends in correspondences especially, and wrote literally thousands of letters to them, often inserting poems in her letters. It was not until her death, however, that the sheer size of her body of work would become

❧ WOMEN WORKING ❧

Emily Dickinson (1830–1886) wrote in a time and place where it was increasingly acceptable for women to make a living on their own. Writing was becoming a respected occupation for women in the upper echelons of society. Louisa May Alcott (1832–1888) amassed a small fortune for her family to live on through her series of books written for young readers. Harriet Beecher Stowe (1811–1896) outsold every American writer, and other writers of the "sentimental" school. Sarah Willis (1811–1872), better known as "Fanny Fern"), not only had a huge best seller of fiction, but also made more money as a journalist for the New York Ledger *than any other columnist writing in 1855.*

Women were also joining the ranks of the working class. The growth of "mill towns"—small urban communities built around a factory, typically a textile mill—created jobs that were often filled by women. Mills in Waltham, Massachusetts, and other mill towns in Massachusetts relied on teenaged girls and young women and provided lodging for them in boarding houses that were carefully supervised. By 1832, in firms with 150 or more employees, the majority of workers were women; in the big textile factories, the figure was more than 80 percent. The girls who worked in Massachusetts and lived in boarding houses viewed their work as temporary, an opportunity to accumulate some savings which would allow them to go west, marry, and claim a small piece of the American dream.

---

known. After Emily's death, her sister Lavinia discovered a cherry-wood cabinet containing well over a thousand poems. Over 800 of them were bound together in hand-stitched little books called "fascicles."

Dickinson's life remains a mystery. Why did she not share these poems in her lifetime? What inspired her during her most productive years? Why was she so reclusive? Who were her loves and lovers? We know something of the events in her life—where she lived, where she went to college, who her friends were—but by and large she lived an uneventful life. Writing quietly in her home in the small village town of Amherst, Massachusetts, she was nobody—at least in terms of a culture that esteems public characters and self-promoting individuals.

Her greatness is readily found in her poetry. However, the poems themselves take on the same mysterious character as her life. The more her readers engage themselves in her poetry, the more they realize they are caught up in a riddle. Like her personal life, the poems are ambiguous, rarely yielding to easy interpretations, categories, or definitions.

How then do we understand Dickinson's place in American literature? In "Self-Reliance," Emerson wrote that "Whoso would be a man must be a nonconformist. He who would gather immortal palms must not be hindered by the name of goodness, but must explore if it be goodness. Nothing is at last sacred but the integrity of your own mind." Dickinson—though not one of the "men" Emerson imagined—was such an individual. Her poetry is at once wholly original, tireless in its search for immortal truths, and yet deeply personal and introspective.

An Intensely Original Poet

One cannot stress enough the originality of the formal aspects of Dickinson's poetry. To a modern reader used to experimentation in poetic technique, it is difficult to see the ICONOCLASM of her poetry. Dickinson defies labels. Her antipathy towards naming—or being named—can be readily seen in almost every poem: she does not title them. She openly defies conventions. She rhymes when she wants to rhyme; her meter can be metronomic, or childishly sing-song, or somber, as in the poem "I Felt a Funeral, in my Brain" (1862), in which one can almost hear the church bells tolling:

I felt a Funeral, in my Brain,
And Mourners to and fro
Kept treading —treading—till it seemed
That Sense was breaking through —

And when they all were seated,
A Service, like a Drum—
Kept beating—beating—till I thought
My mind was going numb—

One can see even in this one small passage some of her signature poetic forms. She has a diction of her own, capitalizing nouns, repeating certain words and phrases for dramatic effect. We see here also the most distinctive feature of her poetry: her unconventional punctuation and her innovative use of dashes.

Dickinson uses her unconventional poetry in much the same way as Whitman: Its purpose is to celebrate the individuality of the poet herself. The two poets, however, could not be any more different in terms of approach to their subject. Whitman's is forever outward and extroverted. Whitman wrote of a thousand Americans seen from the poet's objective gaze. Dickinson's poetry is inward and introverted.

She writes of one American and the thousands of thoughts and observations that enter into one's mind in a lifetime.

The subjects of Dickinson's poems are typically personal themes
that she revisits again and again. She, for example, writes often of
death; in "I heard a fly buzz when I died," she imagines the circumstances of her own death.

> I heard a fly buzz when I died;
>   The stillness round my form
> Was like the stillness in the air
>   Between the heaves of storm.

Though such themes are indeed personal, they are not idle mor-
bid fantasies. For Dickinson, it was important to keep an eye on
death, for it kept one always in mind of what was most important:
the immortal soul. She continues,

> The eyes beside had wrung them dry,
>   And breaths were gathering sure
> For that last onset, when the king
>   Be witnessed in his power.

She describes her own body in decay, but turns to the greater
significance of her death. She speaks of the "last onset," an OXY-
MORON that suggests the duality (and irony) of death: it is last in that
it is death of the mortal body, but it is also an onset in that it is a beginning of the immortal soul's journey toward heaven.

Dickinson uses a number of personal themes in this way. She
delves into issues such as marriage, the place of women in American
society, love, sensuality, the world of spirit, beauty, or romantic nature. However, in all these themes, there is always a turn to the universal experience of all humankind. For Dickinson, all of these
personal concerns are ultimately matters of the soul. By connecting
the meditative poet to this higher spiritual plane, her poems point to
the proper place of introspection, thought, and emotion in all humankind. For Dickinson, the mystery of herself and her poetry invites the
reader into her world, where they will find a higher truth:

> Tell all the Truth but tell it slant—
> Success in Circuit lies
> Too bright for our infirm Delight
> The Truth's superb surprise
> As Lightning to the Children eased
> With explanation kind

Emily Dickinson
Unlike Whitman, only a few images of Emily Dickinson (1830–1886) exist; this likeness is from a family portrait painted when she was a young girl.

The Truth must dazzle gradually
Or every man be blind—

For those readers who search Dickinson's poems to find the character of the poet within them, they will find a ready and able guide, one unafraid to explore the nation within. Although Dickinson would not assume this role for her own generation, she has become a spiritual compass for subsequent generations.

The End of Romanticism

It is an irony that the era of American romanticism ends in 1860, coinciding with the election of the nation's most romantic of heroes, Abraham Lincoln. A month after Lincoln's election, South Carolina attempted to secede from the Union, and the Civil War began in earnest in April 1861. Outside observers of the Civil War were shocked by the ferocity with which Americans killed each other. In one particularly bloody battle, Antietam, an estimated 23,000 Americans were killed or wounded in a single day. With such brutality in the world, it had become difficult to see the beauty in nature and the inherent goodness of the human spirit. The era of American romanticism had come to a violent end.

By the time of the war, the major figures of the romantic movement were of advanced age or dead. William Ellery Channing, Margaret Fuller, James Fenimore Cooper, Horace Mann, and Theodore Parker all died before the Civil War. Thoreau was in bad health at the outbreak of the Civil War and died of tuberculosis in 1862. The survivors did their part for the cause of emancipation. Emerson gave his full support to the Union cause; Whitman worked tirelessly as a Union nurse; Louisa May Alcott also served the Union as a nurse, contracting a lifelong illness for her efforts.

In 1865, a few days after Lincoln's assassination, Emerson delivered a moving elegy at the funeral services held in Concord: "We might well be silent, and suffer the awful voices of the time to thunder to us." However, a romantic in the end, Emerson chooses to honor the principles by which Lincoln lived, seeing even in the darkest hours the triumph of the good:

There is a serene Providence which rules the fate of nations,
which makes little account of time, little of one generation or
race, makes no account of disasters, conquers alike by what is
called defeat or by what is called victory, thrusts aside enemy
and obstruction, crushes everything immoral as in-human, and
obtains the ultimate triumph of the best race by the sacrifice
of everything which resists the moral laws of the world.

TIMELINE

Science, Technology, and the Arts	Literature	History
1803 First successful steam engine built in England	Emerson born in Boston	President Thomas Jefferson makes Louisiana Purchase; Lewis and Clark expedition
1806 Gas streetlights introduced in Newport, Rhode Island	Webster *A Compendious Dictionary of the English Language*	Jefferson orders the arrest of Aaron Burr for conspiracy to commit treason
1812 American Antiquarian Society founded in Worcester, Massachusetts	Byron *Childe Harold's Pilgrimage*	United States declares war on Great Britain
1817 Construction of Erie Canal begins	Hegel *Logic* Bryant "Thanatopsis"	
		Monroe inaugurated as fifth president of the United States.
1819 Jethro Wood granted patent on the iron plow	Irving *The Sketch-Book of Geoffrey Crayon*	Alabama enters the Union as a slave state
1820 Cotton crop 335,000 bales for the year	Channing *The Moral Argument Against Calvinism* Cooper *Precaution*	The Missouri Compromise
	Cooper *The Pioneers*	
1823 First American state geological survey (North Carolina)		The Monroe Doctrine pronounced as U.S. foreign policy
1825 John Stevens builds steam engine for American railways	Bryant "A Forest Hymn" Coleridge *Aids to Reflection*	Mexican government opens Texas to U.S. settlers
1826 First American railroad opens in Quincy, Massachusetts	Cooper *The Last of the Mohicans*	Deaths of ex-presidents Adams and Jefferson on July 4th
1827 In Salem, Massachusetts, Dixon establishes a factory for the manufacture of lead pencils	Cooper *The Prairie* Poe *Tamerlane and Other Poems*	New York state officially abolishes slavery; 10,000 slaves freed
1828 Audubon publishes first volume of *Birds in America.*	Irving *A History of the Life and Voyages of Christopher Columbus* Hawthorne *Fanshawe* Alcott *Observations on the Principles and Methods of Infant Instruction*	Andrew Jackson elected president
1830 Cotton crop for the year, 732,000 bales	Channing "The Importance and Means of a National Literature"	Jackson signs Indian Removal Act; Webster and Hayne slavery debates

1835 Morse builds the first American telegraph	Channing *Slavery* Hawthorne "Young Goodman Brown"	Attempted assassination on President Jackson
1836 Colt patents revolver and opens gun factory in Connecticut	Alcott *Conversations with Children on the Gospels* Emerson *Nature* Emerson "The American Scholar"	Siege of the Alamo; Sam Houston elected first president of Republic of Texas
1837 Blacksmith John Deere of Vermont develops the steel plow for the frontier farmer	Hawthorne *Twice-told Tales* Poe *The Narrative of Arthur Gordon Pym of Nantucket* Whittier *Poems Written During the Progress of the Abolition Question*	Panic of 1837 (global economic crisis); Martin Van Buren succeeds Jackson as president
1838 First steamship crosses the Atlantic	Channing "Self Culture" Emerson "Divinity School Address" De Tocqueville *Democracy in America* (U.S. edition)	Removal of Cherokee Indians from Georgia; 4,000 die on the "Trail of Tears"
1840 Cotton crop, 1,348,000 bales	Alcott "Orphic Sayings" Poe *Tales of the Grotesque and Arabesque* Emerson and Fuller Transcendentalist journal *The Dial*	World Anti-Slavery Convention held in London
1841 Establishment of Brook Farm Institute of Agriculture and Education	Cooper *The Deerslayer, The Pathfinder* Emerson *Essays: First Series;* Poe "The Murders in the Rue Morgue"	President William Henry Harrison dies after one month in office; succeeded by John Tyler
1842 Dr. Crawford Long of Georgia first to use anesthesia in an operation	Emerson "Man the Reformer" Poe "The Masque of the Red Death" Whitman *Franklin Evans or the Inebriate*	Ohio representative Joshua Giddings, censured for mentioning slavery, resigns his seat
1844 Gasoline engine patented by Stuart Perry	Emerson *Essays, Second Series* Hawthorne "The Artist of the Beautiful"	Texas Annexation Treaty signed by the United States and Texas, providing for admission of Texas as a U.S. territory
1845 First publication of popular science journal *Scientific American*	Poe *The Raven and Other Poems* Margaret Fuller *Woman in the Nineteenth Century*	Great Irish potato famine; President James K. Polk introduces manifest destiny, beginning aggressive expansion to West

1846 Smithsonian Institution is founded in Washington, D.C.

Thoreau moves to Walden Pond

Douglass *Narrative of the Life of Frederick Douglass*

Hawthorne *Mosses from an Old Manse*

Poe "The Cask of Amontillado"

Melville *Typee*

Fuller *Papers on Literature and Art*

U.S. declares war on Mexico; President Polk negotiates Oregon Territory treaty with Great Britain

1849 Regular steamboat service from the East Coast to the West Coast begins; Elizabeth Blackwell becomes first American woman doctor

Thoreau "Resistance to Civil Government," *A Week on the Concord and Merrimack Rivers*

Poe dies in Baltimore

California gold rush begins; Polk dies after leaving office; Zachary Taylor becomes 12th U.S. president

1850 The founders of the Waltham Watch Company perfect the manufacturing process necessary for mass assembly of precision components

Melville *Redburn, Mardi*

Hawthorne *Scarlet Letter*

Melville "Hawthorne and His Mosses"

Emerson *Representative Men*

Margaret Fuller dies

Zachary Taylor dies in office, succeeded by Millard Fillmore; Fugitive Slave Law passed; Compromise of 1850

1851 The Erie Railroad completed, connecting the Great Lakes with New York City, thus competing with the Erie Canal as a transportation route

Hawthorne *House of Seven Gables*

Melville *Moby Dick*

Henry Rowe Schoolcraft *Historical and Statistical Information Respecting the History, Condition, and Prospects of the Indian Tribes of the United States*

James Fenimore Cooper dies

John C. Calhoun publishes proslavery position in *A Disquisition on Government and a Discourse on the Constitution and Government of the United States*

1852 The Studebaker Brothers wagon company founded, which will later pioneer motor vehicles

Stowe *Uncle Tom's Cabin*

Melville *Pierre*

Hawthorne *The Blithedale Romance*

Louisa May Alcott *Flower Fables*

Thoreau *Walden*

Massachusetts institutes compulsory education

1854 The ambrotype replaces the daguerreotype as a cheaper alternative to photography

Franklin Pierce elected president; Dorothea Dix advocates mental health reform bill, passed by both houses, but vetoed by Pierce

1855 J.A. Roebling, designer of the Brooklyn Bridge, completes Niagara Falls suspension bridge

1859 Darwin publishes *The Origin of Species*

1860 The Pony Express relay mail system makes its first run

Whitman *Leaves of Grass*
Longfellow *The Song of Hiawatha*
Melville *Benito Cereno*

Thoreau "A Plea for Captain John Brown"
Stowe *The Minister's Wooing*
Evans *Beulah*

Emerson *The Conduct of Life*
Hawthorne *The Marble Faun*
Longfellow *The Children's Hour*

Kansas-Nebraska Act passes; George Fitzhugh publishes *Sociology for the South; or, The Failure of a Free Society*
Supreme Court upholds Fugitive Slave Act; John Brown leads attack on Harpers Ferry in Virginia and is hanged
Abraham Lincoln elected president; South Carolina secedes from Union

GLOSSARY OF TERMS

abolitionist a person in favor of doing away with a law or an objectionable practice, such as slavery

aesthetic relating to the appreciation of art and beauty

Calvinism Christian theology based on the teachings of John Calvin, which emphasizes God's grace for the elect, predestination, and original sin

capitalism economic system in which wealth is controlled by private individuals and corporations

Civil War U.S. conflict that occurred from 1861 to 1865 between the northern states, known as the Union, and the southern states, known as the Confederacy; also called the War between the States

classical a style of or relating to ancient Greek and Roman art, architecture, or literature

commodity an article of trade or commerce

commune a group of people or families who live together and share everything

Enlightenment philosophical movement of the eighteenth century characterized by reason, humanitarian principles, and resistance to traditional dogma

ensemble band or group of individuals, such as musicians, playing together as a unit

epic a long narrative poem, heroic and episodic in nature, celebrating grand and majestic events

Federalists proponents of the Federalist political party (1787) who believed in the establishment of a strong federal government

Free Soil Party U.S. political party (1847–1854) that opposed the extension of slavery into any new American territories

free verse poetry that does not fall into a regular or formulaic rhyming scheme or meter

Fugitive Slave Law (1850) proslavery law that gave southern plantation owners the legal right to recapture escaped slaves in free states

fundamentalism religious viewpoint characterized by a return to fundamental or conservative principles, such as a literal interpretation of the bible

genre classification of artistic, musical, or literary composition characterized by a particular form, style, or content (epic, novel, tragedy, etc.)

Gothic romance literature popular in the late eighteenth and nineteenth centuries emphasizing the grotesque and mysterious

Great Chain of Being belief in the order of the universe, whose chief characteristic is a strict hierarchal system from God down to the lowest living creature

grotesque a style of art which includes natural forms and monstrous figures

hack journalist person employed to write on dull or trite subjects as defined by a publisher

hubris excessive pride in one's abilities or achievements

iambic meter common English metrical foot in which an unaccented syllable is followed by an accented one, as in "around" and "a-bout"

iconoclasm a break with or disdain for established dogmas or conventions

intuition understanding that comes through immediate perception, without the conscious use of reasoning

Kansas-Nebraska Act (1854) controversial law that overturned the Missouri Compromise and paved the way for expansion of slavery into new territories

kosmos also "cosmos," referring to the universe as a whole; also used to indicate universal harmony

laissez-faire doctrine that economies do best when governments do not interfere with free markets

Louisiana Purchase (1803) U.S. acquisition of lands from France which more than doubled the size of the country and opened up the Western frontiers for exploration and settlement

mechanism doctrine that all natural phenomena may be explained by material causes and mechanical principles

metaphysical relating to the spiritual nature of reality

Missouri Compromise (1820–21) agreement between pro- and antislavery states concerning the extension of slavery into new territories

Monroe Doctrine (1823) principle of American foreign policy calling for an end to European intervention in the American hemisphere

neo-Calvinism nineteenth-century artistic and intellectual movement that sought to unite Calvinistic thought with contemporary political and social issues

neoclassicism revival of the ancient models of Greek perfection and classical correctness

nonconformist one who does not ascribe to accepted social conventions, traditions, or customs

Original Sin Christian belief that Adam and Eve's sin in the Garden of Eden created an inherently sinful nature in all humankind

oxymoron a figure of speech that presents a contradiction in terms, such as "jumbo shrimp"

pantheist person who tolerates and worships all gods and believes God is present in all natural forces

perfectionism conviction that moral and spiritual perfection is attainable in this life

personalism doctrine that emphasizes the rights of the individual person

Pilgrims group of English Puritans who settled in America, crossing over on the Mayflower in 1620 and arriving in Plymouth, Massachusetts

primeval relating to the original state or early evolution of humankind

rationalism belief that truth may be discerned by logic and reason

Republican American antislavery political party founded in 1854 and replacing the Whig party; Abraham Lincoln was the first Republican president

rights of man belief set forth by Thomas Paine that men are born equal and should be free from societal oppression

romanticism a philosophy that asserts the power of the individual and the inherent goodness in nature

romantic movement literary and artistic movement in the late eighteenth and nineteenth centuries which emphasized individuality, beauty in nature, freedom from traditions, and the importance of the senses and feelings

romantic reform social reform movements of early to mid- nineteenth century America which sought to promote social justice, equality, and education

sublime greatness that is awe-inspiring, majestic, and transcendent

temperance organized efforts to induce people to abstain from alcoholic beverages

Transcendentalism idealistic and visionary philosophy that upholds the belief of a spiritual, intuitive reality rather than one based on mundane experience

Upanishads, The a collection of sacred Hindu mystical texts

War of 1812 war between the United States and Great Britain, 1812–15

Whig Party major U.S. political party, begun in 1834 in opposition to the Democratic-Republicans and disbanded in 1854 over the issue of slavery

BIOGRAPHICAL GLOSSARY

Alcott, Amos Bronson (1799–1888) New England philosopher and educator. A visionary, Alcott was known for educational experiments, such as the utopian community of Fruitlands. He ran a number of progressive schools for children in his lifetime, including the Temple School in Boston with Elizabeth Peabody. However, his freethinking ideas often led him into conflict with parents, and his forays into education were largely unsuccessful. In May 1843, Alcott tried his hand at creating a utopian educational community called Fruitlands. The small community did not prepare adequately for the winter that year and disbanded early in 1844. Alcott had better success as a philosopher. While his "Orphic Sayings" in *The Dial* (1840–1844) were widely ridiculed, Alcott later published a philosophical treatise called *Tablets* (1868) that was better received critically. Alcott maintained a long career as a lecturer, through which he promoted Transcendentalist ideas in public "conversations." At the end of his career, he had his greatest educational success with the Concord School of Philosophy and Literature, established in 1879. Alcott died in 1888 and was buried in the famed Sleepy Hollow Cemetery.

Alcott, Louisa May (1832–1888) New England novelist, author of best-selling *Little Women* series. The daughter of Bronson and May Alcott, Louisa May was often on the receiving end of her father's educational experiments and the subsequent economic troubles that followed for her family. She wrote of the spartan Fruitland experiment in the satirical article "Transcendental Wild Oats" (1873). In order to offset her family's economic hardships, Alcott worked as a tutor and writer. Despite early rejections by publishers, Alcott broke through with *Hospital Sketches* (1863), based on her experiences as a nurse during the Civil War. Her greatest success, however, came when she tried her hand at the children's book market with *Little Women* (1868). The story of the March sisters growing up in nineteenth-century New England made Alcott, at the age of 35, one of the most popular writers in the world. She followed with a number of sequels, *Little Women: Part Second* (1869), *Little Men* (1871), and *Jo's Boys* (1886). A prolific writer, Alcott's books amassed a small fortune, securing financial stability for her family. She died in 1888, two days after her father.

Brown, John (1800–1859) Controversial abolitionist who led a failed slave revolt at Harpers Ferry, Virginia, in 1859. Brown's radical intention was to secure a military stronghold where runaway slaves could find refuge. He was captured by General Robert E. Lee, and his trial and execution made him a martyr for the antislavery movement. He was defended by Thoreau in "A Plea for Captain John Brown" (1859) and eulogized by Emerson in two separate speeches. Vilified in the South and martyred in the North, Brown's raid polarized the nation and became one of the most significant events leading up to the Civil War.

Calhoun, John C. (1782–1850) U.S. Senator from South Carolina and vice president (1825–1832). Calhoun was elected as vice president under John Quincy Adams and Andrew Jackson but clashed with both over both personal and political issues. He was widely seen as Jackson's heir apparent to the presidency but was passed over for Martin Van Buren in Jackson's second term. In 1832, Calhoun returned to the Senate, where he became a vocal proslavery advocate. Calhoun defended slavery under the argument of "state's rights," which he outlines in the posthumous treatise *A Disquisition on Government and a Discourse on the Constitution and Government of the United States (1851)*. Revered in the South after his death in 1850 as a symbol of southern political ideals, his likeness was used on the currency for the Confederate States of America.

Calvin, John (1509–1564) French theologian. His idea of predestination, that God elects certain souls for salvation, influenced American protestant theology, especially the early Puritans. In nineteenth-century America, the two major strains of Calvinism were represented by the Congregationalists and Presbyterians. Congregationalism was for a time the leading religion in America, but declined in popularity by mid-century. Based directly on Calvinist doctrine, the Presbyterian Church grew throughout the century. However, the church split on the issue of slavery in 1861 and was not reunited until 1983. Calvinist principles, especially the concepts of original sin, conversion, damnation, and the apocalypse influenced the Baptists and Methodists, two of the fastest growing religious movements in nineteenth-century America.

Channing, William Ellery (1780–1842) Boston Unitarian minister. A liberal Christian humanist and intellectual, Channing greatly influenced the ideas and social reform movements of the Transcendentalists. Through his sermons and writings, Channing defined many of the principles of the early Unitarian church. In his open "Letter to Rev. Samuel C.

Thacher" (1815), Channing ignited the "Unitarian Controversy," which effectively divided the orthodox Calvinists and liberal Christians. In a "Sermon on War" (1816), Channing outlined the moral necessity for all Christians to oppose war. In "Likeness to God" (1828) and "Self Culture" (1838), Channing asserted his beliefs in individualism and the perfectibility of human beings. He argues that all human beings should aspire to improve themselves and live up to their potential, creating in their own souls the likeness of God's perfection. Channing's ideas pervaded the artistic and intellectual movements of the early nineteenth century, influencing the likes of Henry Wadsworth Longfellow, Frederic Henry Hedge, Theodore Parker, Dorothea Dix, Elizabeth Peabody, Horace Mann, and Ralph Waldo Emerson. Channing was a vocal opponent of slavery until his death in 1842.

Cole, Thomas (1801–1848) American landscape artist and acknowledged father of the Hudson River School. An English immigrant, Cole came to America in 1818 and was drawn to the beauty of its landscape. He moved to New York, where he could find a market for his paintings. There, he met Asher B. Durand (1796–1886), with whom he would collaborate for much of his life. The growing number of artists painting in and around in New York led to a movement known as the Hudson River School, which included such painters as Sanford Robinson Gifford (1823–1880), Frederic Edwin Church (1826–1900), John Kensett (1816–1872), Albert Bierstadt (1830–1902), and Worthington Whittredge (1820–1910). Cole's landscapes are noted for their romantic scenes of nature, in which he would juxtapose unusual subjects, such as Christian symbols, Native Americans, or classical architecture.

Cooper, James Fennimore (1789–1851) Upstate New York novelist, author of *The Leatherstocking Tales.* Cooper is best known for his stories of Native Americans and early frontier life. Between 1813 and 1819, all four of James Fenimore Cooper's brothers died, as did his mother. Two of his children also died, both just under two years of age. Cooper turned to writing, partly as a response to these tragedies. Cooper's literary career spanned the period from 1820 to his death, in which time he produced roughly 32 novels, two biographies, four histories, a textbook, a memoir, and a series of European travel guides. He gained his greatest popular success in the series of books known as *The Leatherstocking Tales.* Cooper wrote the first, *The Pioneers,* in 1823, and quickly followed up with *The Last of the Mohicans* (1826) and *The Prairie* (1827). He resumed the series in 1840 with *The Pathfinder,* which was then followed by *The Deerslayer* (1841). Cooper was one of the few American writers in his day who received both popular and critical acclaim. His ability to synthesize American history and ideas of democracy with romantic fictional characters, plots, and settings made him the first great American novelist.

Dickinson, Emily (1830–1886) New England poet. Unknown until after her death, Dickinson became an icon of American poetry, known for her innovative style and sensitive treatment of universal themes, such as death, isolation, love, God, and nature. Most of Dickinson's poetry was published posthumously (she published a few poems in her lifetime, but anonymously). She had written in seclusion most of her life, occasionally inserting her poems into letters to friends and relatives. It was not until after her death in 1886 that her sister Lavinia discovered hundreds of poems hand-stitched together in manuscript "fascicles." Though the poems were undated and untitled, Lavinia made it her life's goal to publish and publicize her sister's poetry. She turned the poems over to Mabel Loomis Todd, who edited and published them in three editions in the 1890s. Dickinson's literary achievement was soon recognized, and her literary reputation escalated throughout the twentieth century. Today, she is acknowledged as being one of the most influential poets of the modern era.

Emerson, Ralph Waldo (1803–1882) New England philosopher, and father of Transcendentalism. Emerson's life was punctuated by personal tragedies: His father died when he was eight; he lost all three of his brothers; his first wife Ellen; and, at the age of 20, his eldest son, age five. Nevertheless, he maintained a positive outlook throughout his life that pervaded his philosophy as well as his close friendships with a great number of artists, thinkers, and theologians. Emerson's household in Concord, Massachusetts, was a center of intellectual activity, out of which grew the so-called Transcendental Club (1836), a gathering of a wide variety of New England intellectuals. The members included the likes of Frederic Henry Hedge (1805–1890), William Ellery Channing (1780–1842), Theodore Parker (1810–1860), George Ripley (1802–1880), Amos Bronson Alcott (1799–1888, the poet Jones Very (1813–1880), Henry David Thoreau (1817–1862), Margaret Fuller (1810–1850), journalist Orestes Brownson (1803–1876) and Nathaniel Hawthorne (1804–1864). These meetings led to the publication of the Transcendentalist journal *The Dial* (1840–1844), which Emerson edited with Margaret Fuller. Emerson maintained a lifelong career as a lecturer and public speaker. A former Unitarian minister and teacher, Emerson spoke eloquently on the basic principles of Transcendentalism, such as self-reliance, nature, and equality. His lectures served as complements to his publications, which include *Nature* (1836), *Essays I* (1841), *Essays II* (1844), *Representative Men* (1850), *English Traits* (1856), *Conduct of Life* (1860), and *Society and Solitude* (1870). As a public figure, Emerson spoke out against slavery and delivered powerful eulogies for John Brown and Abraham Lincoln that were widely circulated at the time. No other American thinker of the nineteenth century so deeply affected the direction of the social, political, and cultural movements of his day.

Fuller, Margaret (1810–1850) New England intellectual and woman's rights activist. [Sarah] Margaret Fuller (1810–1850) was born in Cambridgeport, Massachusetts. Her father was a lawyer and congressman, known for his sternness toward his children. At her father's behest, Fuller received a rigorous education. At a time when few women were given formal education, Fuller was far more learned than most of her male contemporaries. She befriended Emerson and together they founded *The Dial* (1840–1844), a literary and philosophical journal. The critic Perry Miller in his *The Transcendentalists: An Anthology* (1950) describes Fuller as having "a passionate nature with which the males in the Transcendental group were ill-equipped to cope." In nineteenth century America, middle-class women were supposed to be moral educators to their children and supporters of their husbands; they were supposed to preside over the domestic realm, while keeping out of public culture and politics; and they were supposed to be models of civility and decorum. Margaret Fuller was none of these. She was an ambitious author, publicly outspoken, and a superior intellectual. It is thought that the strong character of Zenobia in Nathaniel Hawthorne's *The Blithedale Romance* is modeled on Fuller. She and her family died tragically in a shipwreck off Fire Island, New York, in 1850.

Hawthorne, Nathaniel (1804–1864) New England novelist. Hawthorne was born into a prominent Puritan family. His father, a sea captain, died when Hawthorne was four. Hawthorne and his mother moved to Maine, where they lived an isolated, reclusive life. Hawthorne was an ambitious writer early on in his career but could not support himself financially. He was given a job at the Boston Customhouse by his college friend Franklin Pierce. Hawthorne would later write a biography of Pierce for his presidential campaign. Hawthorne befriended many in the Transcendentalist intellectual community, and in 1841, he was one of the principles of the utopian Brook Farm community. His stay there was short-lived, however, as he clashed with various members of the group. In 1842, he married Sophia Peabody. Sophia's sister Elizabeth, a publisher and a central figure in Boston intellectual life, helped Hawthorne secure the connections he needed for his literary career. Hawthorne gained notoriety for *Mosses from an Old Manse* (1846), written while staying at Emerson's "Old Manse" estate. Hawthorne then published his two masterpieces, *The Scarlet Letter* (1850) and *The House of the Seven Gables* (1851), both of which were critically acclaimed. Hawthorne broke with his Transcendentalist friends, publishing the Brook Farm satire *The Blithedale Romance* in 1852. That year, his literary support of the proslavery Franklin Pierce created a further rift, especially among his wife's family. Hawthorne was given a consulship position in England under the Pierce administration and remained in Europe over the next seven years. He died unexpectedly in New Hampshire on a trip to the mountains with Pierce in 1864.

Irving, Washington (1783–1859) New York writer, author of "The Legend of Sleepy Hollow" and "Rip Van Winkle." Early in his career, Irving made a name for himself writing satires, such as *Salmagundi* (1807) and *A History of New York* (1809), by and large humorous observations of New York City society and American politics. In 1815, Irving moved to England to help with the family business (hardware), but it failed. Under the advice of the famed Scottish author Walter Scott (1771–1832), Irving turned to fiction writing. He began writing a collection of travel stories and observations of English life through an American point of view. He also began gathering folk tales, which he turned into short stories of an American character, such as "Rip Van Winkle" and "The Legend of Sleepy Hollow." In 1819, he published the entire collection of writings in *The Sketch Book of Geoffrey Crayon*. The book was enormously popular, making Irving one of the first American authors to gain international fame. Irving went on to write other "sketch" books on the western frontier, as well as the biographies *History of the Life and Voyages of Christopher Columbus* (1828) and *The Life of George Washington* (1855).

Jefferson, Thomas (1743–1826) Third president of the United States. One of the most versatile intellectuals ever to occupy the White House, Jefferson held a wide range of interests ranging from music, to classical literature, architecture, religion, and philosophy. An advocate of individual rights, Jefferson was the chief author of the Declaration of Independence. As president, Jefferson opposed the Federalists, believing that the federal government was best at dealing with foreign affairs, while state and local governments were better suited for implementing local laws. An agrarian, Jefferson oversaw the Louisiana Purchase in 1803, which more than doubled the size of the United States at that time. A scientist and naturalist, Jefferson promptly sent Meriwether Lewis and William Clark to explore and report on the new territory. A philosopher, Jefferson believed in reason, which enabled him to address the political controversies of his day with calm diplomacy. He is largely credited with putting the nation on a solid political path during a critical period of the its history.

Kant, Immanuel (1724–1804) German philosopher. Kant's belief that the mind contains universal truths outside the realm of experience deeply influenced the romantic movement in Europe. Moreover, it was Kant's "Transcendental Idealism," which Emerson borrowed for the basis of American Transcendentalism. In "The Transcendentalist" (1842), Emerson writes, "It is well known to most of my audience, that the Idealism of the present day acquired the name of Transcendental, from the use of that term by Immanuel Kant, of Konigsberg, who replied to the skeptical philosophy of Locke, which insisted that there was nothing in the intellect which was not previously in the experience of the senses, by showing that there was a very important class of ideas, or imperative forms, which did not come by experience, but through which experience was acquired; that these were intuitions of the mind itself; and he denominated them "Transcendental" forms. The extraordinary profoundness and precision of that man's thinking have given vogue to his nomenclature, in Europe and America, to that extent, that whatever belongs to the class of intuitive thought, is popularly called at the present day "Transcendental."

Longfellow, Henry Wadsworth (1807–1882) American poet. Longfellow was a professor of modern languages and taught at both Bowdoin College (1829–1835) and Harvard (1836–1854). Longfellow achieved international literary fame through narrative poems such as *Evangeline* (1847), *The Song of Hiawatha* (1855), *The Courtship of Miles Standish* (1858), and *Tales of a Wayside Inn* (1863). He was the most popular American poet of his day, largely because of the accessibility of his poetry, which appealed even to children, and his ability to create unique American myths out of historical figures. Two years after his death, Longfellow was the first American poet to be memorialized in the Poet's Corner of Westminster Abbey.

Melville, Herman (1819–1891) New England novelist, author of *Moby Dick*. A seaman in his youth, Melville transformed his experiences into seafaring adventures that explored the conflict between nature and humankind. Melville's first two novels *Typee* (1846) and *Omoo* (1847), both set in the South Seas, were financial successes. However, his third novel *Mardi* (1849) did poorly. In fact, none of Melville's subsequent novels would approach the success of his first two. *Moby Dick* (1851), one of the great American novels, was neither a critical nor popular success. His novel *Pierre* (1852) was a dismal failure. Melville's struggles in finding an audience demoralized him. Financial hardships forced him to sell his farm in 1866, and he stopped publishing novels. He died in poverty and obscurity. His last novella *Billy Budd* was published posthumously in 1924. About this time, his work underwent a critical revival. In the course of the twentieth century, Melville gained a reputation as one of the great American novelists.

Poe, Edgar Allan (1809–1849) Southern short story writer and poet, author of "The Raven," "The Tell-tale Heart," and "The Purloined Letter." Poe's writings typically explore the dark recesses of the human psyche. Poe's personal life mirrored his dark imagination. Orphaned as a child, he was raised in Richmond, Virginia, by his godfather John Allan, a wealthy businessman, with whom Poe did not get along. As a young man, Poe continued to run into trouble and was expelled from both the University of Richmond and West Point. In 1835, Poe became the editor of the *Southern Literary Messenger*. He married his 13-year-old cousin Virginia Clemm in 1836, and left his job at the *Messenger* in 1837. Over the next ten years, he took positions at four different magazines, but continued to write fiction. In 1847, Virginia died, after which Poe reportedly attempted suicide. In 1849, he died under mysterious circumstances in Baltimore. Like so many others, Poe's literary reputation grew after his death. Many scholars, interested in the relationship between psychology and art, were drawn to Poe in the twentieth century. His dark stories continue to be popular reading today.

Thoreau, Henry David (1817–1862) New England philosopher, author of *Walden* and *Civil Disobedience*. Thoreau sought to unite Transcendentalist philosophy with a pragmatic, socially responsible way of life. In 1837, the 20-year-old Thoreau began a lifelong friendship with Emerson, who, fourteen years his senior, acted as his mentor. Thoreau benefitted greatly from Emerson's contacts, and was a regular attendee at Emerson's Transcendental Club meetings. In 1842, Thoreau's brother John died of lockjaw. Wanting to get away and to make sense of the tragedy, Thoreau moved to Walden Pond, near Concord, building a cabin in the woods on a piece of land owned by Emerson. There, Thoreau wrote *A Week on the Concord and Merrimack Rivers*, a story of a trip he and his brother John had once taken. During that time, he also kept a journal that documented his philosophy of living simply and closely to nature. In 1854, Thoreau published *Walden, or a Life in the Woods*, which established him as one of the leading Transcendentalist thinkers of his day. Thoreau became increasingly outspoken against slavery, and his plea for the abolitionist John Brown placed him at the center of a political firestorm in 1859. Thoreau died in 1864 of tuberculosis and was eulogized by his friend Emerson. Many of Thoreau's works were published posthumously, resulting in Thoreau's growing popularity in the twentieth century. Thoreau's *Civil Disobedience* (1849) influenced political protest movements, especially nonviolent resistance to unethical government practices. *Walden* has since become the most widely read of all the Transcendentalist writings.

Whitman, Walt (1819 1892) New York Poet, author of *Leaves of Grass*. Born in Long Island in 1819, Whitman was not formally educated. He worked as a journalist and printer for many years; he also tried his hand at school teaching and carpentry. Sometime in the late 1840s, inspired by Emerson, Whitman began writing *Leaves of Grass*. Writing in unconventional meter and rhythm, Whitman explored in his poem the diversity of life experiences in democratic America. In 1855, he published and promoted the poem at his own expense. The poem received mixed critical reviews and the poem's risqué sexual themes were offensive to many. Undaunted, Whitman continued to revise it throughout his lifetime, completing nine editions. Eventually, the poem began to garner a wider audience. During the Civil War, Whitman served the Union as an army nurse working in a field hospital in Washington, D.C. His experiences there resulted in the book of poetry *Drum Taps* (1865). At the time of his death 1892, he had established a solid literary reputation and popular following. Today, he is universally regarded as one of the greatest American poets.

FURTHER READING

Chapter 1. The Intellectual and Social Foundations of Romantic Thought

Abrams, M. H. *The Mirror and the Lamp: Romantic Theory and the Critical Tradition.* New York: Oxford University Press, 1972.

Barzun, Jacques. *Classic, Romantic, and Modern.* Chicago: University of Chicago Press, 1975.

Bowra, C.M. *The Romantic Imagination.* New York: Oxford University Press, 1961.

Honour, Hugh. *Romanticism.* New York: Westview Press, 1979.

Kermode, Frank. *The Romantic Image.* New York: Routledge, 2002.

Chapter 2. Romanticism and the New Nation

Gilmore, Michael. *American Romanticism and the Literary Marketplace.* Chicago: University of Chicago Press, 1985.

Lawrence, D.H. *Studies in Classic American Literature.* 1923. Cambridge: Cambridge University Press, 2003.

Lewis, R.W.B. *The American Adam: Innocence, Tragedy, and Tradition in the Nineteenth Century.* Chicago: University of Chicago Press, 1955.

Matthiessen, F.O. *American Renaissance: Art and Expression in the Age of Emerson and Whitman.* New York: Oxford University Press, 1941.

Novak, Barbara. *Nature and Culture: American Landscape and Painting, 1825–1875.* New York: Oxford University Press, 1980.

Porte, Joel. *The Romance in America.* Middletown: Wesleyan University Press, 1969.

Smith, Henry Nash. *Virgin Land: The American West as Symbol and Myth.* Cambridge: Harvard University Press, 1950.

Chapter 3. Transcendentalism

Boller, Paul. *American Transcendentalism, 1830–1860, An Intellectual Inquiry.* New York: Putnam, 1975.

Buell, Lawrence. *Literary Transcendentalism.* Ithaca: Cornell University Press, 1973.

Jehlen, Myra. *American Incarnation: The Individual, The Nation, and The Continent.* Cambridge: Harvard University Press, 1986.

Marx, Leo. *The Machine in the Garden: Technology and the Pastoral in America.* New York: Oxford University Press, 1964.

Richardson, Robert D. *Emerson: The Mind on Fire.* Berkeley: University of California Press, 1995.

Chapter 4. The Literature of Romantic Reform

Andrews, William L. *To Tell a Free Story: The First Century of Afro-American Autobiography, 1760–1865.* Champaign: University of Illinois Press, 1988.

Douglass, Ann. *The Feminization of American Culture.* New York: Anchor Books, 1988.

Parrington, Vernon L. *Main Currents in American Thought: The Romantic Revolution.* New York: Harcourt Brace, 1930.

Schlesinger, Arthur. *The Age of Jackson.* Boston: Little, Brown, 1945.

Swift, Lindsay. *Brook Farm.* Secaucus: The Citadel Press, 1961.

Thernstrom, Steven. *A History of the American People: To 1877.* New York: Harcourt Brace, 1988.

Chapter 5. The Critical Romantics

Chase, Richard. *The American Novel and Its Tradition.* Baltimore: John Hopkins University Press, 1980.

Fiedler, Leslie. *Love and Death in the American Novel.* Chicago: Dalkey Archive Press, 1997.

Levine, Lawrence W. *Highbrow/Lowbrow: The Emergence of Cultural Hierarchy in America.* Cambridge: Harvard University Press, 1988.

Miller, Perry. *Errand into the Wilderness.* Cambridge: Belknap Press, 1956.

Tompkins, Jane. *Sensational Designs: The Cultural Work of American Fiction, 1790–1860.* New York: Oxford University Press, 1986.

Chapter 6. Romanticism and Poetic Voice

Anderson, Charles. *Emily Dickinson's Poetry: Stairway of Surprise.* Westport: Greenwood, 1982.

Capper, Charles. *Margaret Fuller: An American Romantic Life: The Private Years.* New York: Oxford University Press, 1994.

Calhoun, Charles C. *Longfellow: A Rediscovered Life.* Boston: Beacon Press, 2005.

Feldman, Paula R. *Romantic Women Writers: Voices and Countervoices.* Lebanon, NH: University Press of New England, 1995.

Reynolds, David S. *Whitman's America: A Cultural Biography.* New York: Vintage Books, 1996.

INDEX